TOWN HOUSE ARCHITECTURE

David J. Eveleigh

SHIRE PUBLICATIONS

Published in Great Britain in 2011 by Shire Publications
Ltd, Midland House, West Way, Botley, Oxford OX2 0PH,
United Kingdom.

44-02 23rd Street, Suite 219, Long Island City, NY 11101,
USA.

E-mail: shire@shirebooks.co.uk   www.shirebooks.co.uk

A CIP catalogue record for this book is available from the
British Library.

Shire Library no. 629.   ISBN-13: 978 0 74780 832 9

David J. Eveleigh has asserted his/her right under the
Copyright, Designs and Patents Act, 1988, to be identified
as the author of this book.

Designed by Tony Truscott Designs, Sussex, UK
and typeset in Perpetua and Gill Sans.

Printed in China through Worldprint Ltd.

11 12 13 14 15   10 9 8 7 6 5 4 3 2 1

COVER IMAGE
Eighteenth-century houses on St Michael's Hill, Bristol.

TITLE PAGE IMAGE
Pebble-dashed walls on a terraced house in Glenfrome
Road, Horfield, Bristol, built in 1931. The treatment of
the exterior paintwork, with a dark colour for the window
frames and doors, and light cream or white for the
window casements, is typical of the period.

CONTENTS PAGE IMAGE
St Andrew's Place, Regent's Park, London, by John Nash,
built 1823–6.

ACKNOWLEDGEMENTS
Archidave, cover and page 20; Steve Blake, pages 10 and
24 (top); Birmingham Archives and Heritage Service,
page 19 (bottom); Black Country Living Museum, page 39
(top); Bristol City Museum and Art Gallery, page 46
(bottom); Bristol Record Office, pages 32 (top), 33, 34,
47 (left) and 71 (top); Cheltenham Art Gallery &
Museum, pages 22, 23 (top), 27 (bottom) and 55 (top);
The Late Duncan Marshall, pages 23 (bottom), 24
(bottom), 25 (bottom), 40, 45, 48, 49 (bottom), 54 (top),
64 (top), 72 and 73; Nottingham City Council, page 51;
Paolo Margari (paolomargari <http://flickr.com/
paolomargari), page 72; Jonathan Taphouse
(www.taphousephotography.com), page 8;
The Victoria & Albert Museum, page 7; West Yorkshire
Archive Service, © Leeds City Council, pages 31 (top) and
70. All other pictures are from the author's collection.

Additionally, I would like to thank Steve Blake and Stephen
Price for making invaluable comments on the text. The
book is dedicated to the memory of Duncan Marshall,
Senior Lecturer in The Faculty of Environment &
Technology at The University of the West of England,
Bristol (1953–2009) who suggested that I should write a
brief 'architectural flypast' of town house styles: out of
that idea came this book.

Shire Publications is supporting the Woodland Trust, the UK's leading woodland conservation charity, by funding the dedication of trees.

CONTENTS

A NEW STYLE, 1640–1714

THIS IS a brief history of urban housing in Britain – of the ordinary and commonplace housing of large cities and towns, of seaside towns and old market towns, new towns and suburbia. But why begin in the mid-seventeenth century? Why not earlier? After all, many British towns and cities are considerably older; some contain houses of earlier date. The story could be taken further back in time, but, if we start from our present-day perspective, we can, with little difficulty, trace many familiar elements of the British townscape and its housing stock to the mid-seventeenth century, when a whole new approach to domestic architecture emerged: the replacement of tradition with fashionable taste, and of local ways of thinking – and building – by universally recognised canons of design that were not British but Italian.

Architectural and social historians – like all historians – claim 'watersheds' in history at their peril. But the arrival of a new approach to town house architecture and property development can be identified with remarkable ease to a particular building venture. The date was the 1630s; the architect was Inigo Jones (1573–1652), Surveyor General to the King; and the location was Covent Garden, London, on land belonging to the fourth Earl of Bedford. Here Jones designed a piazza, or formal square, filled on two sides with desirable residences; in 1945 Sir John Summerson claimed this to be 'the first great contribution to English urbanism'. Inigo Jones also laid out Lincoln's Inn Fields, linked to Covent Garden by Drury Lane. Then, after the Restoration in 1660, Southampton Square – the first by name in London – was developed by the fourth Earl of Southampton; it was later renamed Bloomsbury Square. Leicester, Soho and Golden Squares followed in the 1670s, and St James's Square was completed by 1680.

From the building of these new residential areas three clear features emerged. The first was estate development by landowners (many of whom in London were aristocratic), who leased their land to speculative middlemen or builders in return for a ground rent; these men built the houses, usually to the landlord's specification, and, when the lease expired, the land and buildings reverted to the landlord. This process of leasing and building was

Opposite:
Lindsay House,
Lincoln's Inn Fields,
London, c. 1640,
by Inigo Jones.
The façade has
a rusticated
basement and
Ionic pilasters
rising to the attic
storey. From Colen
Campbell, *Vitruvius
Britannicus*.

to become the fundamental pattern that shaped the growth of London and other towns and cities for the next two hundred years. The second consequence was the creation of socially exclusive suburbs of high-quality housing. In London the building of fashionable streets and squares in Westminster resulted in the creation of the West End, inhabited by the rich and supported, inevitably, by luxury shops and an army of tradesmen and servants. In Bristol the western suburb of Clifton developed as a place where the residents – typically members of the gentry, senior Anglican clergy, admirals, army officers, professional and literary people – enjoyed the fresh air, clean water and pleasant views across the Avon to Somerset.

The terms of the building leases usually ensured that 'noxious trades' were excluded, but there was a price to pay for this exclusivity and this was the creation of industrial suburbs, where a working population lived cheek by jowl with trade and industry. Such was London's East End, which had begun to spread outwards along Whitechapel High Street by 1700. Districts such as Bethnal Green were to become bywords for urban squalor. Mean streets containing housing of the worst quality, poorly constructed, damp, dilapidated and overcrowded – and invariably short of safe water and decent sanitation – created an environment where poverty, crime and disease flourished. The presence of industries, such as glass and brick making, leather tanning and soap boiling, which were often excluded elsewhere, ensured that the industrial suburb was usually enshrouded in perpetual smoke.

But to return to the world of the wealthy property developer, the third important development concerns architecture, and here the intervention of Inigo Jones was vital. He introduced to England from Italy an entirely new creed of architecture that set new conventions of aesthetics and style derived from a Renaissance reinterpretation of the ancient architecture of Greece and Rome. It was also an architectural discipline that became the basis of a new profession – that of the architect (Inigo Jones is frequently hailed as Britain's first). Moreover, this new 'classical' style of architecture was to become universal. This was also new: a set of widely published rules and laws that applied equally to the large country mansion and the small town house of four or six rooms.

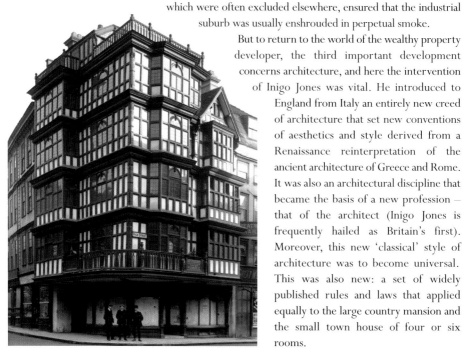

The 'old order of architecture', represented here by the Dutch House, Bristol, built c. 1676. This five-storey timber-framed building is seen in c. 1909 following a comprehensive Edwardian restoration. It was destroyed in 1940 during the Blitz.

Jones designed several important state buildings, notably the Banqueting House at Whitehall, as well as his houses in Covent Garden, and all had a strong Italian accent. His particular style is called Palladian and is named after the Italian architect Andrea Palladio (1508–80), who popularised his interpretation of ancient architecture through his writings and his designs for the large villas which dot the countryside around Vicenza. Whilst Jones's contribution was seminal, it was, nevertheless, restricted in impact, but out of these first essays in domestic classical architecture a new style evolved. Although maintaining the sense of Palladian symmetry and proportion, houses built after the Restoration were less obviously Italian in character.

Bloomsbury Square, London, by Pollard and Jukes, 1787.

Outside areas of good building stone, the use of red brick was a distinguishing feature. Building in brick was not entirely new of course, but what was new was the scale of its adoption from the 1660s and 1670s, and its contribution to creating a new style of domestic architecture. The extensive rebuilding of the City of London following the Great Fire of 1666 was carried out in brick. Outside London traditional building methods, relying heavily on timber framing filled with lath and plaster, continued for a while. In Bristol – then one of the largest and most important cities outside the capital – they continued to be used through the 1660s and 1670s; but the new style arrived there in the 1690s, and by 1701 the building of large brick houses in a new formal square, soon to be named after Queen Anne, had begun. Looking back on the reign of Charles II (1660–85), Roger North (*c*. 1653–1734) declared: 'here ended the antique order of housing'. It was not long before several centuries of 'vernacular' house building rooted in local traditions and materials – timber framed construction, gabled roofs and casement windows – succumbed to the new conventions of classical architecture. Classicism was found everywhere, but its hold on English domestic architecture was only complete where money and fashion exerted the strongest hold. Lower down the social scale, smaller houses for the 'lower middling sort' (there was no large-scale building for the poor before the twentieth century) kept elements of the vernacular tradition alive.

Besides the use of brick, several other features came to characterise late Stuart domestic architecture. Roofs were a dominant feature, tall and hipped, with a deep wooden eaves cornice and large chimney stacks. Dormer windows in the roof were another typical feature, although an entire attic storey was occasionally found above the main cornice. Windows were no longer wide and fitted with outwardly opening casements, but upright and, from about the 1680s, fitted with sliding sashes that could be opened without disrupting the classical façade. The two sliding frames usually contained six

29 Queen Square, Bristol, *c*. 1709–11: Flemish-bond brick façade dressed with long and short quoins marking the party walls; superimposed Doric, Ionic and Composite columns, and alternate segmental and triangular pediments placed over carved keystones in the centre of flat window arches; typical wooden modillioned eaves cornice and roof dormers. The doorcase is mid-eighteenth-century.

panes of hand-blown 'crown' glass and these usually varied in proportion according to the dimensions of the window; they were to remain a common feature of British houses down to 1914.

The adoption of classical principles was not confined to the proportions of the basic shell of the house: the façade was frequently embellished by an exuberant, if perhaps naïve, application of a wide range of classical motifs, such as quoins, that is dressed stonework on the corners of walls, and keystones over windows – with a prominent

Giant pilasters, ornate keystones and sills adorn the façade of this early-eighteenth-century house in Waterloo Terrace, Bridgnorth, Shropshire.

centre stone that was often elaborately carved. Stone pediments – variously triangular, 'segmental' (an arc of a circle) or 'broken' – were also widely used over windows, while the front door provided another focal point, dressed with architraves and around 1700 with large shell-hood canopies supported on scrolled 'consoles', or brackets. Some town façades of the early 1700s were further enlivened by the application of fluted pilasters and richly carved capitals. All of these decorative accents in stone contrasted well with the brickwork.

Houses built from the 1660s are sometimes described as Carolean or 'Wren style', acknowledging the influence of Sir Christopher Wren (1632–1723), after Inigo Jones the greatest architect of seventeenth-century England. For the later houses, built from about 1690 to 1715 or 1720, the style is named after Queen Anne, even though her reign lasted just from 1702 to 1714. Today Queen Anne style houses survive in cathedral closes, as in Salisbury, and in picturesque market towns. 'Every old provincial town', observed Sir Banister Fletcher (1866–1953), 'furnishes examples of these quiet and dignified houses, often now occupied by local professional men.'

A semicircular shell-hood with scalloped interior, resting on scrolled consoles and sheltering the doorway of a house built c. 1700 in Bridgnorth.

GEORGIAN, 1714–1815

THE ACCESSION of George I in 1714 was to mark an unusually abrupt change in direction. The following year, the first volume of *Vitruvius Britannicus* by Colen Campbell (1676–1729) was published; two further volumes appeared in 1717 and 1725. Condemning the 'affected' work of foreign architects, this book was hugely influential. It marked a rejection of the free and fanciful interpretation of late-seventeenth- and early-eighteenth-century classicism and a return to a purer form of Palladianism, which was now redefined as a national form of architecture. Thus it was neo-Palladianism which shaped the Georgian architecture that can be seen today in the streets of London, Bristol, Bath, Dublin and Edinburgh, and also in many smaller towns such as Ludlow, Shropshire. It remained the dominant influence throughout the reigns of the first two Georges, up to 1760. For much of this time British politics was dominated by an elite of aristocratic Whig grandees, and their patronage of Palladian architecture was a major reason for its supremacy. Another reason was the support of an influential circle of architects who set down the principles and grammar of neo-Palladianism in pattern books. Neo-Palladianism has been described as 'rule-book architecture' and the emphasis was on order and proportion. As the architect Isaac Ware (1704–66) stated, 'there ought to be a uniformity of all the parts first to the whole building and next to each other'. For several decades these rules were obeyed by fashionable architects and provincial builders across Britain and the result was an extraordinary consistency of style.

The new emphasis on order and uniformity had a far-reaching impact on the townscape. Streets of identical or near-identical houses – many in terraces – created a sense of regularity and consistency of architectural style, in total contrast to medieval and post-medieval urban development. The terraced house arose from the need of the speculative builder to squeeze as many houses as possible into one street. So the typical Georgian town house was tall and narrow, with a long narrow garden or court behind, and, for the largest houses, a coach-house or stable at the rear of the plot served by

Opposite:
The front entrance to 46 Merrion Square, Dublin, begun in 1762. The doorway is framed by Ionic pilasters and side windows; it is surmounted by a wide fanlight typical of Georgian Dublin and found elsewhere in Ireland.

The Royal Crescent, Bath, 1767–74, by John Wood the Younger (1728–82). Comprising thirty three-storey houses overlooking a large sweeping lawn, this was Britain's first crescent and is generally acknowledged to be one of the greatest examples of urban Palladian architecture in Britain. The façade of Bath stone is dominated by the giant Ionic columns supported by a rusticated ground storey.

a subsidiary road or 'mews'. The backyard usually contained a privy or 'bog house' — a primitive sanitary arrangement set over a cesspit or 'bog hole'. All houses except the poorest had basements containing a kitchen, a back kitchen or scullery, and various stores — pantry, larder and storage for coal. The coal store often extended under the pavement so that the coalman could deliver the coal without entering the basement: circular cast-iron coal-hole covers remain a feature of the pavements in many Georgian streets. At the front, the basement often looked on to a deep void below the street called the 'area', which often contained 'area steps', which provided a tradesmen's entrance directly into the kitchen. The plan of the house was usually extremely simple, with one room at the back and one at the front on each floor, with a passage and staircase at one side, although inevitably there were many minor variations on this plan. The party walls of the houses usually contained the chimney flues, which added strength to the structure. Large houses would contain up to twenty-five or more individual flues, which, until the 1840s, were swept of soot by young climbing boys.

The Georgian builder used stone or brick according to local availability. In London the bricks of good, hard quality used for the outer walls were known as 'stocks', whilst poorly made, cheaper 'place' bricks, which included as much ash as clay, were used for the unseen work of party walls and partitions. The stocks used in and around London were of two colours: grey and red. The latter were slightly more costly and often used for lintels and window arches, while the grey bricks were preferred for walling in general. In the late eighteenth century London stocks were almost uniformly a pale, yellowish brown. A fourth, more expensive type of brick was the 'cutting brick', a crimson brick of very fine sandy quality and capable of accurate cutting — hence the name, but it was also known as 'rubbing brick' or

In the eighteenth century there was much reconstruction and refacing of earlier buildings. The mid-eighteenth-century brick façade of 40 Broad Street, Ludlow, Shropshire, hides the late-medieval origins of the house.

'Windsor brick'. In the best work these were used instead of red stocks for window arches and decorative dressings. The Georgian bricklayer almost invariably laid his bricks in 'Flemish' bond, in which the headers and stretchers alternated in each course. After bricks, timber was the Georgian builder's chief material: Baltic fir and oak were widely used, and from about 1720 mahogany gradually came to replace oak for the more expensive items of joinery, including interior doors and stair balustrades. For the paving of the halls of large houses, Purbeck stone was often specified, frequently with little diamonds of black Namur marble at the crossing of the joints. The principal rooms were distinguished by ornate ceiling plasterwork and by white marble fireplaces that contained freestanding 'stove grates' of burnished steel and brass.

Adapting Palladio's principles, the neo-Palladians created a system of proportions and ratios based on the square and circle (or cube

Gauged brickwork was widely used for Georgian window arches, as seen here above the windows of a house in Wendover, Buckinghamshire. Fine red bricks were cut and rubbed to precise shapes and laid in thin lime-putty joints.

An oak staircase with turned balusters and newel posts, decorative brackets and ramped handrail, c. 1740; St Mary's Street, Bridgnorth.

and sphere). The square, in particular, was considered the key to architectural beauty, and Robert Morris (1703–54), in his *Lectures on Architecture* of 1734 and 1736, established seven ideal proportions, all based on the cube. Proportions based on squares were used to determine window openings and the system of window openings relative to wall areas: thus, if the house was three bays wide (the usual width of the Georgian town house), then the space occupied by the first- and second-floor windows would usually be made roughly a square.

For the Palladian façade this system of proportions was combined with the architectural elements of the Roman temple, consisting of a rusticated basement, columns or pilasters, entablature (including the cornice and pediment), and attic. Five types of columns with the superstructure they supported – known as the Five Orders – were used to determine the adornment of the façade. The Five Orders were the Tuscan, Doric, Ionic, Corinthian, and Composite, easily distinguished by the particular carving of the capitals and their individual proportions. The Orders were applied to a building for decorative purposes

The Five Orders of Ancient Architecture: (from left) Tuscan, Doric, Ionic, Composite and Corinthian. From Nicholson's *New Practical Builder*, c. 1824.

and also to 'order' the design of the façade. The Orders were either applied to the façade or implied by dividing the façade in height according to the divisions of an individual column. Even where the main architectural components of the temple were absent, their presence could be implied by the use of certain details. Thus a cornice or even a flat string course was used to suggest the location of the entablature, or a sill band or string course at first-floor level could be used to indicate the line of the column base, while another above the ground-floor windows could be used to mark the junction between the column pedestal and temple podium. In a three-storey house, for example, the temple composition was implied by the ground-floor storey

Albermarle Row, Clifton, Bristol, 1762. The wall of the middle house is brought slightly forward to form a central feature crowned by a triangular pediment. The terrace was built to serve as lodgings for visitors to the Hotwells, the fashionable spa of eighteenth-century Bristol.

corresponding to the area of the podium, while the two storeys above fell within the area of the column shaft. For the largest and grandest terraced block, the temple formula provided further inspiration for the front. By adding a pediment over the centre, the row was given a palace-like front. Now the overall unity of the design was more important than the façades of individual houses. John Wood (1704–54) adopted the palace front for the north side of Queen Square in Bath, started in 1728, and thereafter the pediment was widely used.

While Palladianism encouraged uniformity and consistency, there was still, nevertheless, considerable scope for the details of the façade – particularly the proportions and placing of windows and the designs of doorcases – to evolve during the eighteenth century. Taste and fashion and building controls were the chief determining factors. In order to reduce the risk of fire, in 1707 a Building Act was passed which banned the prominent eaves cornices that had risen to popularity in Restoration London. Instead, the roof was half hidden by a parapet wall with a cornice of brick or stone.

Two years later another Act laid down that the window frames, instead of being nearly in the same plane as the brick face, were to be set back 4 inches, leaving a reveal of brickwork, which gave a sense of solidity to the walls. In the late seventeenth century the ground floor was often treated as the principal storey, but in houses of the early eighteenth century the ground- and first-floor windows are often found to be roughly the same size, while second-floor attic rooms were lit by square windows. The piers between the windows of early-eighteenth-century houses were often considerably narrower than the openings although the early Palladians favoured the reverse ratio, with the piers being considerably wider than the windows. Later, the width of window openings and piers was almost invariably fixed at 3 feet 5 or 6 inches. By the mid-eighteenth century the first floor was established as the main floor, the *piano nobile*, and had the highest ceilings and tallest windows, and the first-floor windows were usually a double square and sometimes given further pre-eminence by the use of

Doorcase with fanlight, from William Paine, *The Carpenter and Builder*, c. 1789.

architraves and full entablatures, as in Bath and Bristol. Then in the late eighteenth century the principal floor returned to ground level.

The main entrance formed the dominant ornamental feature of the façade, although doors were placed symmetrically only on larger houses. For the typical terraced house, the door was almost invariably placed at one side of the façade so that a two-bay room – the parlour – could be located to the side of the entrance and hallway. From the 1720s and 1730s Palladian designs based on the temple were widely used for doorcases with pillars supporting an entablature and pediment. In London porticoes were commonly made of white Portland stone, which formed a striking contrast to the brick walls. Doors were usually of six panels: early ones were tall and filled the entire opening, but in the 1720s the fanlight – a semicircular window over the door – first appeared as a means of allowing light to enter the hall. The entrances of many Georgian town houses were further embellished by delicate wrought ironwork, including area railings and supports for oil lamps, which sometimes formed an arch over the entrance.

Exterior wrought-iron lamp-holder, by W. H. Pyne, 1805.

From the 1760s the strict conventions of Palladianism were challenged and then modified by a new breed of professional architects, of whom the greatest were Robert Adam (1728–92), his younger brother James (1732–94), Sir William Chambers (1723–96) and James Wyatt (1746–1813). Robert Adam was the leading force in creating a new style, spending several years abroad and examining sites of antiquity at first hand. He denounced the eternal repetition of pattern-book architecture and instead introduced a greater degree of flexibility based on the interpretation of the actual evidence surviving from antiquity. Inspired by his study of the ruins of Diocletian's Palace at Split in Dalmatia, he also introduced a new range of decorative motifs. The result was a new architectural style, generally known as 'neo-classical' or even simply as 'Adam style'. It was characterised by buildings with light, elegant lines unbound by strict classical proportion. Rigid and rectangular classical forms were abandoned in favour of curves and ellipses; circular and oval ends to rooms became popular. Adam treated ornament

Windsor Terrace, Clifton, Bristol, attributed to John Eveleigh of Bath. The two centre houses were completed by 1792. Following the bankruptcy of all involved, building resumed in 1808 under John Drew, who reduced the height of the remaining houses and of the pilasters, which fail to meet the cornice.

freely, introducing delicate swags and ribbons in low-relief plaster into his interiors, which were then painted in delicate greens and blues, lilacs, dove greys and faint yellows. Fanlights were a prominent feature of Adam style. They were at the peak of their popularity between 1760 and 1780, when they consisted of a complex pattern in iron and lead, typically of spokes radiating outwards from a central floret and decorated with swags and garlands. Windows were taller, with thinner glazing bars. Lower down the social scale, smaller houses were built to precisely the same proportions, but on a reduced scale. The distinctions were codified in the Building Act of 1774, which aimed at preventing poor-quality construction and reducing the risk of fire. By the Act, houses were categorised or 'rated' according to value and floor area. Each rate had its own code of structural requirements as regards foundations, external and party walls.

From the middle of the century, bay windows, which had been out of fashion since the early seventeenth century, began to reappear. Frequently of timber construction, they were often confined to the ground-floor parlour beside the front door. The roofs of early Georgian houses were tiled, but towards the end of the eighteenth century Welsh slate was widely adopted. After 1750 water closets were installed in the best houses: the houses in the

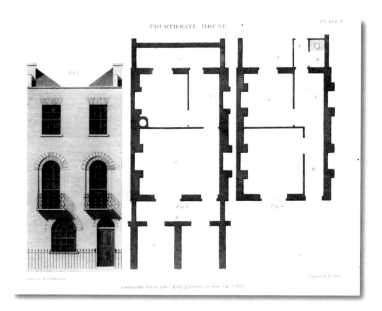

Fourth-rate town house, Nicholson, 1823.

Royal Crescent in Bath had them from new in the late 1760s. From about the same time the freestanding stove grate was replaced by cast-iron hob grates, which filled the chimney opening. These were usually cast with the delicate neo-classical motifs popularised by the Adam brothers, who designed those found on the grates made in the late eighteenth century by the famous Carron Foundry in Scotland.

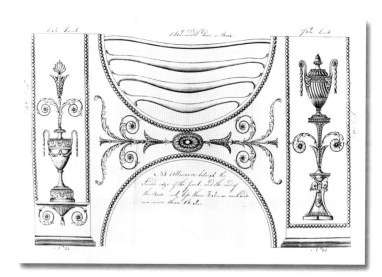

Design for a cast-iron hob grate from the pattern book of Dearman Winwood, Birmingham, c. 1790, showing a profusion of Adam-style decoration.

REGENCY, 1815–40

THE END of the Napoleonic Wars in 1815 marked the beginning of a twenty-year-long building boom, and of a new style of architecture that took its name from the Regency of the Prince of Wales, later George IV, which lasted from 1811 to 1820. In London, large impressive terraces were built by John Nash (1752–1835), the Prince Regent's leading architect, and subsequently by Thomas Cubitt (1788–1855). Elsewhere, the building of Regency housing was on a scale large enough to give such towns as Brighton, Cheltenham, Leamington Spa, and other genteel spa and seaside places, an enduring 'Regency' character. As in London, large, handsome terraces remained a popular form of housing for the well-to-do. In basic plan, these continued to follow the traditional eighteenth-century layout with a basement service area, but the Regency period was also notable for the rise of the detached and semi-detached villa. In the context of British domestic architecture, the term dated from the 1820s when Nash included picturesque villas in his development of Regent's Park, although separate dwellings had been seen in St John's Wood as early as the 1790s. Builders continued to follow well-proven Georgian principles of design and construction – as exemplified by writers such as Nicholson in 1823 – but from the early 1800s house-building took several new directions which were to give Regency architecture its own particular identity.

Regency architecture was, above all, typified by the use of stucco in preference to exposed brickwork. 'Stucco' is a general term used for various kinds of cement coating applied to the external wall of a building. Its use dated from around the time of the Building Act of 1774, when various patent stuccoes were introduced; they were used sparingly until Nash popularised their use in his fashionable developments in London. Several new formulas for 'artificial cements' were developed in the early nineteenth century, when the use of stucco rapidly increased as a means of imitating stone; all respectable stuccoed buildings of the eighteenth and early nineteenth centuries were carefully scored with horizontal and vertical lines to represent stone jointing. The simplicity of a uniform stuccoed façade painted white,

Opposite:
Sun, sea and
stucco in Regency
Brighton: large bay
windows ensure
each house has a
sea view.

Lansdown Court, Cheltenham, designed by Robert and Charles Jearrad was originally known as the Italian Villa and dates from around 1831.

cream or buff provided the perfect foil to the use of plain, slightly projecting bands and restrained ornament. For large terraces, such as Carlton House Terrace, begun by John Nash in 1827, the Orders were still applied. Their façades continued to be arranged in the grand Roman manner with giant columns and pilasters, although the use of lighter accents of ornament came to typify Regency architecture.

Window proportions continued to follow the Georgian model; thin glazing bars still divided sash windows into twelve or more rectangular panes. Doorways continued to be surmounted by fanlights: semicircular designs were still found, but many were now rectangular with delicate vertical muntins that were either arched or angled in imitation of Gothic window tracery. In terraces, the top of the façade was finished in typical Georgian style with an elegant parapet hiding a low roof. Roofs were either pitched at right angles to the front with a central valley, or were of mansard construction, in which case they were aligned to the ridge and tall enough to contain attic rooms with dormer windows looking out over the parapet. Villas were often given low-pitched roofs of gabled or hipped construction with wide projecting eaves. Welsh slate was now the preferred roofing material and formed a striking contrast with the walls when these were of pale-coloured stucco. Some terraces close to the seafront, as at Brighton and Hastings, were built with large sweeping bays so that every house had at least a glimpse of the sea, and elsewhere full-height curved 'bows' became another feature of Regency architecture. Delicate balconies of wrought or cast iron with curving metal roofs resembling Chinese pagodas became popular at first-floor level. Decorative iron trelliswork was also often added to the front entrance, forming a pretty, if flimsy, porch. French windows, which were really glazed doors, opened on to the balconies or, in the case of villas, were placed in rear ground-floor rooms to provide direct access to the garden.

Regency
Cheltenham:
The Crescent –
later and now
known as the
Royal Crescent –
is seen here in a
lithograph of 1821.
It was designed by
the Bath Architect
Charles Harcourt
Masters and dates
from 1805 onwards.

Belvidere Terrace,
The Esplanade,
Weymouth,
Dorset, begun
in 1815.

23

The New Town of Edinburgh is a virtually intact example of Georgian town planning, built in stages from the 1760s to about 1850. Moray Place was built in 1822–36 by James Gillespie Graham (1776–1855). The stone façades have a rusticated ground floor with a giant Tuscan Order of attached columns above.

Regency housing represented a new type of classical architecture that drew on a wider range of sources than ever previously seen. It represented a challenge to the straitjacket of Georgian Palladianism, and the first break with classical restraint can be traced to the emergence of the 'Picturesque' movement in the 1790s. Through the Picturesque, traditional vernacular English forms, continental styles from Italy, France and Switzerland, and

West Mall, Clifton, Bristol, c. 1841: a terrace of twenty-one houses designed by James Foster and William Oakley. The freestone fronts, with their Doric plain-shafted pilasters on the party walls, provide the backdrop to the elaborate Grecian-style verandas at first-floor level.

more exotic elements such as Indian verandas and domed towers were incorporated into Regency domestic architecture – from Nash's fantastical Brighton Pavilion of 1815–23 to the cosy cottages of Blaise Hamlet near Bristol, which Nash also conceived in about 1810. Then, from the early 1800s, through the work of architects such as Robert Smirke (1781–1867), a fashion for Grecian-inspired ornament emerged. Greek Revival architecture found its best expression in large public buildings, but it also found its way into suburban 'villa' development, where large detached and semi-detached houses were dressed up with fluted pilasters and Ionic capitals supporting pediments, and window surrounds and porches decorated with delicately carved Greek-inspired motifs.

Another strong influence that appeared from the 1820s was the 'Gothic', which had first emerged in the mid-eighteenth century. It was a style best

Buckingham Vale, Clifton, Bristol, built c. 1847–50, probably by R. S. Pope. Two houses are brought together behind an Ionic temple front.

Beach House, The Esplanade, Sidmouth, Devon: a superb example of Regency Gothic. Originally built c. 1790, this was the first house on the seafront at Sidmouth and was Gothicised in c. 1826.

A semi-detached
villa of white
Storeton
sandstone at Rock
Park, Birkenhead,
c. 1840.

suited to the small villa or cottage, where a delightfully picturesque effect was achieved by placing doorways and windows in ogee or early Tudor four-pointed arched openings. The windows were filled with delicate Gothic arched glazing bars and leaded lights. These styles were brought together and

A semi-detached
stucco villa at
Rock Park,
Birkenhead. This
quiet, secluded
villa estate for the
'upper middling
classes' was built
between 1837 and
1850. Nathaniel
Hawthorne, the
American writer
and United States
consul in
Liverpool, lived
there from 1853
to 1857; a police
station at the
entrance allowed
no 'ragged or ill-
looking person' to
enter.

Far left: Some of the picturesque embellishments popularised by J. C. Loudon and others, such as pronounced roof gables, ornate chimneys, a pointed 'Gothic' window and Tudor-style drip hoods, are seen on this early-Victorian house in Rock Park, Birkenhead.

Left: A Coalbrookdale hob grate of c. 1840 in an earlier wooden fireplace surround of c. 1790; St Mary's Street, Bridgnorth.

popularised by writers such as John Claudius Loudon (1783–1843). Loudon's highly influential *Encyclopaedia of Cottage, Farm and Villa Architecture and Furniture*, first published in 1833, contained over two thousand designs for houses in a variety of 'romantic' styles: Grecian, Gothic, Old English, Swiss chalet and others. For the supporters of Georgian architecture the appearance of these guides marked a turning point in British building – the start of a 'descent into chaos' as the conventions of Georgian architecture were swept away.

Throughout the first half of the nineteenth century rows of smaller terraces were built in many larger towns close to the centre, but in less fashionable quarters, such as these in St Paul's Street South, Cheltenham, photographed before demolition in the 1930s. The brick fronts retain Georgian features such as the cornice or parapet, and the basement area protected by railings.

VICTORIAN AND EDWARDIAN, 1840–1914

R EGENCY ARCHITECTURE survived Victoria's accession in 1837 and houses with 'Regency' characteristics continued to be built through the 1840s, but gradually and imperceptibly Victorian architecture emerged as a style of its own, shaped by rapid population growth, the influence of new technologies and new materials, and the intellectual input of theorists such as Augustus Welby Northmore Pugin (1812–52), John Ruskin (1819–1900) and William Morris (1834–96). During Victoria's reign Britain's population doubled; the urban-based proportion increased from 54 per cent in 1851 to 79 per cent by 1911, leading to a massive expansion of towns. Speculative builders responded by building suburbs that were sharply delineated by class. Working-class districts were built cheek by jowl with the collieries, mills and factories that provided employment for their inhabitants. The housing generally consisted of rows of tightly packed terraces: although not as fashionable after the 1850s, terraced houses remained the builder's solution to the demand for cheap urban housing until the early 1900s. Economical with land and materials, they were built either back-to-back, so that the rooms had no rear windows, or as through houses, which usually had a two-storey rear extension containing the kitchen and a small third bedroom, and with a privy (or water closet) and coalshed in the backyard. While the back-to-backs and the poorest through houses were completely devoid of any embellishment or ornament, bay windows, moulded brickwork and other details were added to larger terraces that commanded higher rents and had pretensions to respectability. But there was no mistaking the true Victorian middle-class dwelling. Whether detached or semi-detached, these solidly built and substantial houses were large enough to accommodate resident servants, the employment of at least one being a clear indicator of middle-class status.

Whilst a typical working-class house contained between four and six rooms, a large middle-class villa of the 1850s or 1860s could contain twelve rooms or more, with separate family and service areas. The family rooms included bedrooms with adjacent dressing rooms, a water closet but rarely

Opposite:
A view into the crowded backyards of working-class housing in Gustave Doré's well-known engraving of 1872, 'Over London By Rail'.

a bathroom, and large reception rooms with high ceilings, elaborate moulded plaster cornices and marble fireplaces. The servants were usually accommodated in attic rooms while the service area continued to occupy a basement containing kitchen, scullery, pantry and larder, a separate servants' water closet, and, in the largest houses, a housekeeper's room or servants' hall. The houses were private and respectable. They were usually given names that reinforced their grandeur and respectability – 'Albion', 'Richmond' and 'Belmont', for example, and they were usually set back from the road in gardens, which, for the first time since the Middle Ages, became an important part of the urban home environment.

Secluded, private and respectable: a substantial Italianate villa of about 1860 in Clifton, Bristol, with Bath stone ashlar dressings contrasting with the grey Pennant sandstone walls.

Back-to-backs in Leeds, 1 December 1960. Two double-fronted back-to-back houses flanked by yards containing the shared outside toilets. A single toilet cubicle is visible on the left. This area was soon to be demolished and the families relocated under a Leeds City Council slum-clearance programme.

The range of styles available to the Victorian architect helped underline the separateness and individuality of the larger Victorian house. From the 1830s Gothic emerged as the greatest challenge to the dominance of classical styles. Through the influence of Pugin, whose *True Principles of Gothic*

In the nineteenth century seemingly endless rows of terraced houses crossed the scarred industrial landscape of the Black Country. These back-to-back houses dating to the 1850s formerly stood in Brook Street, Woodsetton, West Midlands, where they were home to colliers, farm workers and ironworkers. They are now preserved at the Black Country Living Museum.

The archetypal streetscape of the Victorian working-class suburb: rows of densely packed terraces rubbing shoulders with neighbouring industrial premises. These through houses of the mid-1870s stood in Bridge Street, Barton Hill, Bristol, with the Day Road gasometer in the background.

Opposite: Plan of small terraced houses in Mount Pleasant, Bedminster, Bristol, 1851, with a front best room and a through passage leading to a back kitchen containing a sink and wash copper. The backyard contains a privy and ashpit.

Architecture was published in 1841, a more serious and analytical approach to the use of medieval Gothic architecture emerged. Then, in 1851–3, the art critic John Ruskin published *The Stones of Venice*. This became a key text for the High Victorian Gothic of the middle decades of the century, and through Ruskin's influence elements of the Italian Gothic, including pointed-arched window surrounds, elaborate polychrome brickwork and carved stone decoration, were brought into the leafy suburbs of Victorian Britain. Italian architecture of the sixteenth century was another style that was widely used for large suburban houses in the middle of the century. It had its roots in Regency architecture, when Nash had experimented with a semi-rustic Italianate villa style, and was further developed and popularised in the 1830s by Sir Charles Barry, who drew heavily on the buildings of the Italian Renaissance. Osborne House in the Isle of Wight, designed by Cubitt for Queen Victoria and Prince Albert and completed in 1851, was the grandest example and provided the inspiration for many large villas built in the 1850s and 1860s. Typical features included a square 'belvedere' tower, deep projecting eaves, roof balustrades and round-arched windows. Other styles

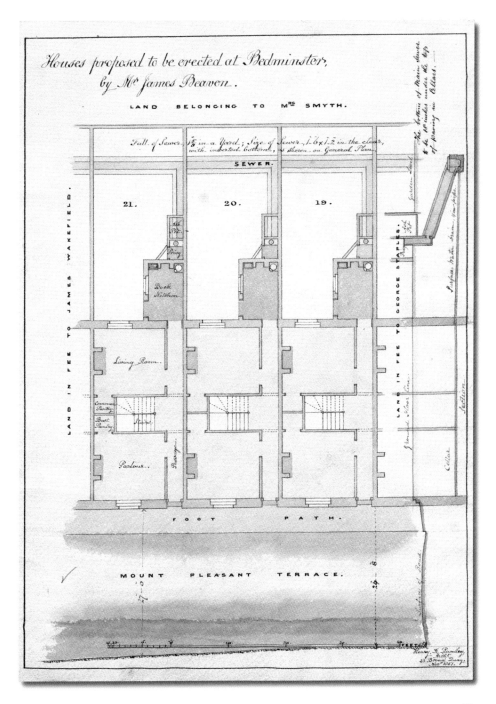

Houses proposed to be erected at Bedminster, by Mr James Beaven.

LAND BELONGING TO MRS SMYTH.

A comprehensive range of service rooms is shown in this plan of the basement of a large detached villa in Pembroke Road, Clifton, Bristol, 1863.

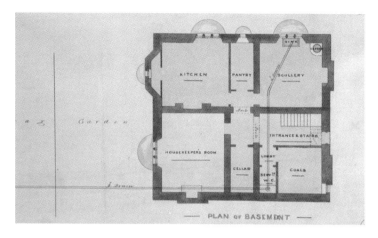

A substantial detached villa, Pembroke Road, Clifton, Bristol, c. 1860.

found included the Northern European, typified by the use of the curved or Dutch gable; the French baroque, which contributed the mansard roof; and Elizabethan and Jacobean, with features borrowed from the typical 'Jacobethan' large house, including towering chimneys, mullioned windows and four-pointed arched front doorways.

These various styles posed a major challenge to the neo-Palladian rules of geometry and proportion: in place of broad sweeps of wall surface, with windows cut in simply and sharply, there was a new emphasis on anything picturesque – on the 'charming character of the irregular'. Architectural historians write of the 'Battle of the Styles', but it was usual for an architect to select a particular architectural style according to the whim of the client. Styles were also amalgamated and motifs mixed so freely in a profusion of detail that it can be difficult to distinguish between the various revivals. But, whatever the choice or mix of styles, the popularity of certain features provided some common characteristics.

Victorian Gothic in brick. A large late-nineteenth-century detached house in Bebington Road, Rock Ferry, Birkenhead, with pointed Gothic windows, two-storey bays and embattled 'belvedere' tower.

Large bay windows, often of two or three storeys and with heavily ornate surrounds, became a dominant feature of the façade after 1850. The bay window contributed to the picturesque quality of the front, but from the inside it offered more space and light – and better views. The halving of the window tax in 1832 and its repeal altogether in 1851 encouraged the use of large windows. They were usually filled with large areas of glass, made possible by the perfection of 'Improved Cylinder Glass' by Robert Lucas Chance in 1832. Sash windows remained standard in the mid-Victorian house but the availability of large sheets of cheap glass resulted in larger individual panes and fewer glazing bars. An entire sash could be filled

Fireplace in a house in Fishponds, Bristol, built in 1861, with the cast-iron arch plate grate in its original marbled slate surround.

First-floor bay window with Venetian Gothic window arches with polychrome and moulded brickwork and carved stone capitals; late nineteenth century; Bebington Road, Rock Ferry, Birkenhead.

with one sheet of glass and, because of the greater weight, the frame of the sash had to be made thicker and strengthened with full mortise and tenon joints at the corners, giving rise to the 'horns', the vertical extensions to the styles that appeared on sashes after about 1840. On larger early and mid-Victorian houses, the windows were often fitted with internal wooden shutters, while roller blinds to keep direct sunlight out of rooms were frequently added to the exterior; many of the ornate wooden blind boxes survive and can be seen framing the upper part of the window opening.

Victorian sash with strengthening horns on the frames; Bridgnorth, Shropshire.

The prominence of the front bay had a curious effect on the position of the front door of larger mid-Victorian houses: it was sometimes found relegated to a less prominent position – even a side wall. By the 1850s the commonest type of front door had four panels in place of the typical Georgian six-panel door. Door furniture tended to be heavily ornate and made of cast iron; following the introduction of the Penny Post in 1840, it usually included a letter box.

Exterior window blinds, 1875.

LAVERTON & CO'S IMPROVED VENETIAN AND OUTSIDE WINDOW BLINDS.

INSIDE VENETIAN BLINDS, PAINTED ANY COLOR, price 8d per Square Foot.

Above: Four-panelled Victorian front doors at The Laurels, Dudley Road, Tipton, West Midlands, c. 1895.

Above right: Cast-iron letter box, late nineteenth century.

Roofs became another integral part of the façade. They were generally pitched steeper and featured hips and gables embellished with elaborate wooden bargeboards and ornate ridge tiles and finials. Multi-storey bays were usually given their own turret-like roofs joined to the front pitch of the main roof. Slate remained the commonest roofing material across much of Britain. Chimneys were also now regarded as a positive feature of the overall design: they were generally tall and decorated with projecting courses of brickwork, stone carving and other ornament reflecting the overall style of the house. This extended to the chimney pots, which were made in a wide range of decorative designs, each with its own particular name, such as 'crown' or 'bishop'; some incorporated elaborate projections to counter down draughts. All these features, of course, added to the picturesque quality of the architecture, which was further enhanced by a return after the mid-century to the use of undisguised red brick and, in stone areas, rubble walls. From the 1860s the use of ornamental brick and terracotta – clay baked at very high temperatures to produce a material claimed to be stronger than brick or stone – became popular for detailed embellishments, although later generations were to condemn the Victorian love of manufactured detail ornament.

Gradually, a reaction set in to the mixed classical and Gothic styles of mid-Victorian architecture, and to the artificiality – and perceived ugliness – of machine-made building parts and fittings. The result was the emergence of the Arts and Crafts Movement, which created a new aesthetic approach in all fields of design, based on a search for greater 'truthfulness' and simplicity in design. In domestic architecture it led to the rise of two new styles, 'Old English Revival' and 'Queen Anne', although in practice the two styles often merged. Old English Revival arrived as a challenge to the accepted order in 1859, when Philip Webb (1831–1915) designed Red House at Bexleyheath, Kent, for William Morris. Rejecting machine-made decoration, Morris and his circle of friends made some of the fittings, including the stained glass and

Above left: Red chimney pots from the catalogue of Hinton, Perry & Davenhill, of Pensnett, West Midlands, c. 1925.

Above: Roof finials from the same catalogue.

The return of brick: this detached house, the former vicarage to St Edmunds Church, Castle Hill, Dudley, was probably built in the 1850s. The strong horizontal lines of the eaves and the rounded window arches show Italianate influences.

Arts and Crafts inspired housing in Downs Park East, Henleaze, Bristol, c. 1900.

tiles, themselves. The house was built of red brick with a high-pitched, red-tiled roof, and incorporated such romantic features as a turret, oriel windows and gables. It marked a return to the vernacular tradition of building and became, in the words of John Cloag, 'the progenitor of a new school of domestic architecture'. Much imitated, it became a dominant influence on the so-called 'stockbroker belt' housing – large detached houses built mainly in southern commuter villages such as Gerrards Cross, Buckinghamshire, up to 1939.

The Queen Anne style evolved in the late 1860s at the hands of a group of young architects who sought to restore the idea of comfort and practicality to domestic architecture. It was pioneered by several architects, of whom W. Eden Nesfield (1835–88), R. Norman Shaw (1831–1912) and J. J. Stevenson (1831–1908) were most prominent. It was never a straightforward revival of the domestic architecture of Queen Anne's reign. While the application of red brick, hipped roofs, tall chimneys, small-paned sashes and white-painted woodwork were motifs borrowed from English domestic architecture of the period 1690–1710, the Queen Anne style that came to public attention in the early 1870s also drew from English farmhouse vernacular, using tile-hung gables and chimney stacks rising from the side of the house. Seventeenth-century Flemish architecture was another source of inspiration: tall, curved and stepped 'Dutch' gables became popular, relieved with horizontal bands of different-coloured brickwork; a common decorative motif was the sunflower in moulded brick panels, whilst in the detailed ornament of the interiors there was even a smattering of Japanese style.

But in terms of layout and function the Queen Anne house of the 1870s was forward-thinking. Windows were placed where they were needed – to provide light within a room, and not just to satisfy the requirements of the façade. On the first floor the dressing room was replaced by a bathroom with fitted bath, wash basin and water closet. J. J. Stevenson, in his *House Architecture* of 1880, was one of the first architects to promote the idea of the freestanding pedestal water closet, which was rapidly adopted from the mid-1880s. Fireplaces, often embellished with Japanese-inspired decoration, were often of the 'slow-combustion' type, which was designed to burn more efficiently and generate less smoke. Another departure from long-established conventions was the abandonment of the gloomy basement kitchen in favour of one located on the ground floor. As a result, the ground-floor plan was larger and usually included three reception rooms, with the third described as the 'morning room' or 'breakfast parlour'.

The Queen Anne style was essentially a middle-class style confined to the large detached or semi-detached home for the well-to-do. One of the greatest expressions of Queen Anne architecture was the development of Bedford Park, Chiswick, west London, from 1876. Several architects were

An 1870s bathroom, from S. Stevens Hellyer, *The Plumber & Sanitary Houses*, 1877.

IMPROVED REGISTER GRATES,

Typical slow-combustion grate of the 1890s with Arts and Crafts inspired tiled side panels.

involved but it was Shaw who gave the estate its overall character. With its winding, tree-lined roads and mixture of house designs, Bedford Park has been hailed as the first garden suburb. In the same decade Shaw and other architects working in the Queen Anne style were also responsible for the designs of large houses of several storeys that line many of the streets of Chelsea and Kensington. They mix Queen Anne motifs with Dutch gables and large, tall windows. Osbert Lancaster (1908–86) was later to call this 'Pont Street Dutch'. There were also a few early experiments with middle-class flats in this style: they were often called 'mansions' – like the massive Albert Hall Mansions in Kensington, designed by R. Norman Shaw and built around 1879. After 1850 philanthropic societies funded the building of a few blocks of flats or tenements to house industrial workers, but in Scotland tenement

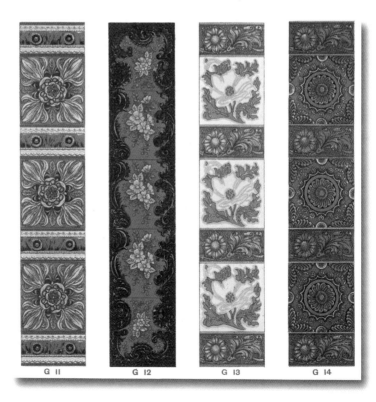

G 11   G 12   G 13   G 14

Fireplace tiles, c. 1895.

Large houses with tall gabled façades in bright red brick were built in Chelsea and Kensington through the late 1870s and 1880s. These terraced houses in Chelsea were designed by R. Norman Shaw.

life was common for many town dwellers in the nineteenth and early twentieth centuries. They were not confined to the poor: the Tenement House, a red sandstone block in Buccleuch Street, Glasgow, for example, built in 1892 and now preserved by the National Trust for Scotland, provided 'respectable' accommodation with a well-equipped kitchen and bathroom supplementing the living room and bedroom.

In the 1890s a new interpretation of the Old English Revival emerged through the work of C. F. A. Voysey (1857–1941) and Sir Edwin Lutyens (1869–1944). In some of his country houses Lutyens combined classical style with the use of local materials, as at Heathcote, Ilkley, West Yorkshire. The houses of Voysey and his followers, built in the early 1900s for wealthy clients,

43

struck a modern look with their low-ceilinged rooms, horizontal windows, roofs sweeping down almost to ground level, and white roughcast or pebbledash walls, although Voysey always saw himself as an architect working firmly within the traditions of British vernacular architecture; his use of pebbledash, for example, came from the traditional harling of Scotland and Cumbria.

From the 1880s through to the early 1900s Shaw's work was much imitated by speculative builders for middle-class housing, and large, fussy, red-brick houses with white-painted timber porches, balconies and verandas, small window panes in the upper sashes, and the occasional Dutch gable, became a familiar part of the outer suburbs of London and other large towns and cities. In the early 1900s the range of traditional motifs applied to the façades of middle-class villas widened: thus pargeting (decorative relief plasterwork), recalling the seventeenth-century domestic architecture of Essex and Suffolk, became popular, as did half-timbered gables, and pebbledash made its debut in suburbia. In the hands of speculative builders, suburban villas began to look like enlarged cottages. Although roofs were prominent, houses were generally not as tall, and there was now a greater horizontal look to the façade. Plans tended to be squarer and, now there was no basement, the main living rooms had direct access to the garden. The hallways were typically wide and spacious, with a porch door filled with stained glass. The porch and hallway floor were often finished with thick unglazed encaustic tiles by Minton or Doulton, whilst moulded and glazed coloured tiles were used for skirtings, dado rails and panels. There was also a revival of late-eighteenth-century style: fireplace surrounds were sometimes dressed with Adam-inspired urns and swags. But the influence of Voysey was also felt and set a simpler, more restrained tone to interiors after 1900. Simple fireplaces with frames of dark oak or brick filled with brightly coloured tiles became popular, while the grate was frequently decorated in the Art Nouveau style, which was to be seen on other interior fittings in the early 1900s. Some of these features found their way down to the better-quality artisan terraced houses built until 1914. Often with their own names in imitation of larger houses, these were villas within a terrace;

Etched-glass porch-door window, Bebington Road, Rock Ferry, Birkenhead; late nineteenth century.

with their bay windows, terracotta ornament and tiled porches, they provided homes for the upwardly mobile artisan and clerk – like the fictitious Mr Pooter of The Laurels, Holloway, London.

For urban mass housing the terraced house of between four and six rooms remained universal. From the 1870s the quality of working-class terraced housing was significantly improved by legislation at local and national level, aimed chiefly at improving standards of public health. Better standards of construction and sanitation and the provision of adequate space, front and back, were enforced through local by-laws, and in many towns in the Midlands and the North the building of new back-to-backs was made illegal, although a national ban was not introduced until 1909. Streets were made wider. Individual through houses were provided with better light and ventilation and better services, including gas lighting and cast-iron ranges in the kitchen. Sanitary provision also improved dramatically in the 1870s, although the systems adopted by local authorities varied considerably: in the South the water closet was widely adopted but until the end of the nineteenth century most Midland and northern towns relied on the dry conservancy system, using ash privies or pail closets. In northern towns it was common to find a narrow back alley running between parallel rows of houses, which was often reached by a narrow passage or tunnel through the terraced block. Access to the backyard enabled local authorities to undertake the regular

Large two- or three-storey terrace houses with heavily bargeboarded gables, two-storey bay windows and roof dormers are found in many resorts popular in Victorian and Edwardian times. These, in Bank Street, Keswick, Cumbria, are built of local Lake District slate and red sandstone and show a profusion of decoration in timberwork, ashlar and terracotta.

A 'fish-tail' gas burner, the ubiquitous gaslight of the nineteenth-century town house.

A building gang outside new terraced houses in Maple Road, Horfield, Bristol, c. 1894. The two-storey bay houses are faced with grey Pennant sandstone and ashlar window and door surrounds.

collection of the waste by municipal dustmen. Everyday life in these houses was usually confined to the rear of the house, facing the backyard; at the front, the parlour was reserved for best and looked on to a made-up street, paved and drained, and lit by gas.

Typically laid out in straight, monotonous streets with little open space, working-class terraced housing was heavily criticised by architects and social reformers. In 1905 Hermann Muthesius wrote of their 'deadening uniformity' and said: '…anyone approaching London above the roofs of these little houses has only to glance at this sea of dwellings to feel something of the misery that seems to prevail here.' It was in this sea of dwellings, typically found on the approaches by rail to many Victorian town and city centres, that elements of the vernacular tradition still survived and merged with 'polite' architecture to create the characteristic small terraced house of the period 1850–1914. The basic order of the façade – the placing of windows

Decorative plaster bracket in the hallway of 7 Rosebery Terrace, Clifton, Bristol, built 1893–4.

Hall passage at 65 Elmdale Road, Bedminster, Bristol, photographed in 1956. Built in 1901, this terraced house has an inner front door glazed with ruby, blue and etched glass, and a decorative arch supporting the first-floor bedroom wall.

and doors – and the proportions of the openings came from formal architecture. Windows continued to be long and vertical and fitted with sashes, and the use of stone lintels or brick arches above the windows – usually either half-round or segmental – conveyed the idea of a classical architrave.

The vernacular element came in local preferences for stone or brick: thus yellow-grey stock brick in London, 'white' in East Anglia, and silver grey in Reading, which was also famous for its decorative

A small open-fire range in 5 John Carr's Terrace, Clifton, Bristol, a terrace block built around 1878.

polychrome brickwork. Elsewhere the brick was red although it was sometimes combined with cream and Staffordshire blue bricks for decorative effect. From the 1880s smooth, bright-red pressed bricks such as those made in Ruabon, North Wales, were widely adopted. The Accrington pressed brick was widely used in Lancashire, but north of Bury and east of Accrington brick gave way to millstone grit, a coarse-grained sandstone. On the Pennines, in mill towns such as Rawtenstall, Burnley, Nelson and Colne, the rows of stone terraces are seen climbing steep slopes with inclined eaves and ridges running parallel to the ground.

Terraces of soot-blackened millstone grit also created the Victorian townscape of West Yorkshire, of towns such as Halifax, Huddersfield, Bradford, Brighouse and Cleckheaton. In Bristol, where houses were built on steep inclines, the individual houses within terraces were always stepped and, until the 1870s, each house was separated by a vertical division in stone. Also in Bristol there was a strong tradition of stone masonry, and so

A rear alleyway running between houses in Albion Street and Albion Place, Chester; late nineteenth century.

the bays and door surrounds were done in ashlar and ornamented with carved decoration. In Birmingham and the neighbouring towns of the Black Country, timber bays, sometimes with elaborate carved work, were more typical. A particular characteristic of the late-Victorian terraced houses of Swansea was the use of low-relief wavy patterns in stucco in the door lintels and keystones of window arches. This feature can be seen on the small houses filling the gridiron of narrow streets in the Sandfields district, west of the city centre. In Norwich rubbed brickwork continued to be used after 1850 for the round-arched doorways and flat window arches, characteristic of the city's small terraced houses. In a few places, such as Hull, Norwich, Bristol and Bridgwater, the continued use of clay pantiles provided further local diversity. The vernacular tradition could make itself felt in other ways, such as the occasional use of casement windows in the small windows of the rear extension, and the various arrangements found for kitchens, sculleries and privies. In the Midlands and the North, separate wash-houses containing a wash copper, sink and sometimes a range were common, although in the West Midlands these backyard structures were generally known as 'brewhouses', which in the local dialect was shortened to 'brew'us'.

Towards the close of the nineteenth century a more radical approach to working-class housing emerged from two entirely different directions. The first can be traced to the 1840s and 1850s, when a number of industrialists

Through terraced houses in Albion Street, Chester, late nineteenth century.

Right: Timber bay window with segmental heads to the sashes and dentils in the cornice: a design probably dating to *c*. 1890, illustrated in a joinery catalogue of 1920.

Far right: Timber bay windows, Dudley Road, Tipton; late nineteenth century.

No. 1080.

No. 1081.—DOUBLE CASED BAY,

and entrepreneurs assumed responsibility for the provision of accommodation for their employees. From 1842 the Great Western Railway provided small Jacobean-style stone cottages for workers brought into the new railway town of Swindon, while in West Yorkshire two millowners, Sir Titus Salt and Sir Edward Ackroyd, built new model villages at Saltaire, Copley and Ackroydon. In the Wirral, Price's Patent Candle Company provided housing at Bromborough Pool in 1852. The quality of the accommodation contained in these early developments varied: the railway cottages in Swindon were cramped and sanitary arrangements were

Anne Hathaway's Cottage for the industrial worker: Port Sunlight, Wirral, was developed from 1889 by William Hesketh Lever to house his company's employees. It set new standards for mass housing that were to influence suburban developments for much of the twentieth century. These of *c*. 1925 in Queen Mary's Drive are by J. Lomax Simpson.

50

primitive; the houses at Copley were back-to-backs. But the decision of Sir William Hesketh Lever (1851–1925) to create a model industrial village at Port Sunlight, near Birkenhead, for his employees in 1889 marked a major advance in terms of architectural design and urban planning. Over a thousand houses were built in a variety of styles and materials, set in a pleasant environment of village greens and tree-lined roads that recalled Blaise Hamlet and Bedford Park. From 1893 a similar scheme was begun south of Birmingham, where George Cadbury (1839–1922) created Bournville.

The second direction came from the Utopian vision of one man, Ebenezer Howard (1850–1928). In his seminal work published in 1898, *Tomorrow: A Peaceful Path to Real Reform*, he promoted the idea of a garden city where urban life might be filled with fresh air, recreational

No Man's Yard,
Sneinton,
Nottingham,
c. 1912.

space and sunlight. From these theoretical beginnings he founded the Garden Cities Association in 1899 and then in 1903 work began on creating a new town at Letchworth, Hertfordshire, with low-density housing in the cottage vernacular, with gardens, and set in tree-lined roads. Other new developments followed: Hampstead Garden Suburb from 1907, and Welwyn Garden City, where building commenced in 1920. In the early 1900s the two strands merged through the involvement of two architects and planners, Raymond Unwin (1863–1940) and Barry Parker (1867–1947); working together, they designed the model village of New Earswick, York, for Joseph Rowntree (1836–1925) and then worked on the designs for Letchworth and New Hampstead Village. Following the First World War, the idea of the garden city or 'village suburb' was to remain a guiding force in the planning of urban housing – of inter-war council estates and post-war new towns – for another half-century.

BETWEEN THE WARS, 1918–39

THE FIRST WORLD WAR marked a watershed in British house construction. For the first time the large-scale provision of working-class housing became the responsibility of the state, while the building of middle-class homes for owner-occupiers was subject to new pressures, such as the arrival of electricity, the spread of the motor car and the expansion of a servantless lower middle class. The building of the new council estates and the development of middle-class suburbs by private developers in the inter-war period were both heavily influenced by the Tudor Walters Report published by the Local Government Board in 1918. Raymond Unwin was its chief author and through him the idea of the garden city movement was brought to the forefront of national housing policy. Together with expert opinion provided by specialist groups, including women's organisations, the report set the die for the creation of entirely new house types.

House-building had come to a virtual standstill during the First World War, creating an acute shortage of housing nationwide. The government brought in a Housing Act in 1919 which required local authorities to assess their housing needs and make good any deficiency with the assistance of a generous government subsidy. The Addison Act was replaced by Housing Acts of 1923 and 1924, and further acts that promoted the construction of council houses were passed in the 1930s. Guided by Unwin's recommendations, the idea was to create garden villages or garden suburbs, and so the estates were to incorporate a mixture of house types in a relaxed setting with no more than twelve houses per acre. A simple cottage style was generally preferred, with gabled, red-tiled roofs, brick walls combined with white render or pebbledash, and horizontal casement windows. Houses were built in pairs or in short terraced runs of up to about five. They were generally low and wide; roofs were hipped, and chimneys low and squat. Gardens, front and back, were usually of generous dimensions. The neo-Georgian style, which had appeared before 1914, was also widely used for the council estates; it was typified by the use of red brick, simple Georgian-style doorcases and small-paned windows.

Opposite:
A Type D detached house in The Drive on the Metropolitan Railway's Weller Estate, Amersham. It was on the market in 1930 for £1,200.

The village suburb: Hillfields, Bristol's first council estate, built from 1919.

The typical privately built 1930s semi-detached house: two-storey bay, red-tiled roof and green-painted gable with an oriel window over the front door; Southdown Road, Westbury-on-Trym, Bristol, c. 1935.

The plan of the typical inter-war council house was generally rectangular: the rear extension, typical of Victorian terraced houses, was abandoned to ensure the back received as much light as the front. Houses were divided into parlour and non-parlour types but they were all provided with a scullery, bath and indoor water closet. There were also experiments with non-traditional building methods, such as the use of metal frames, cast iron or concrete, as a means of reducing costs, although these constructional techniques brought their own problems, such as poor insulation and condensation. The council estates built as a consequence of slum clearance projects in the 1930s reduced standards of accommodation with the building of more non-parlour houses.

If the creation of the council estates was in part a Utopian vision to create a healthy, pleasant home environment for

Early council houses in St Mark's Estate, Cheltenham, from 1919.

ordinary people, the economies imposed on the quality of the houses resulted in heavy criticism of the monotony of the architecture and the setting. By the mid-1930s some large authorities, including the London County Council, Liverpool, Manchester and Leeds, had turned instead to the building of council flats. By the late 1920s the construction of flats was beginning to gain strong support from architects of the Modern Movement, who were inspired by the large apartment blocks for workmen built in Vienna in the 1920s. Gradually the idea of living in multi-storey accommodation began to gain wider acceptance. In London flat-building exceeded cottage-building for the first time in 1936, while in Leeds the giant Quarry Hill scheme entailed the replacement of two thousand slum dwellings with 938 flats from 1938.

Oxford's first council estate was the Gipsy Lane Estate, Headington, consisting of 101 houses built in the London Road; by 1930 the number of houses, including these neo-Georgian examples, had risen to 314.

By 1939 1.1 million council houses had been built, but this figure was outstripped by the 2.8 million middle-class homes built by speculative builders from 1923, when private house-building resumed after the war. The rate of building increased in the early 1930s, reaching a peak in 1936, when 370,000 houses were completed. The commonest house type was the three-bedroom semi-detached, although developments often included detached houses and bungalows. The bungalow came into its own between the wars. Whilst some were built in pairs, the detached bungalow was common and this provided an affordable way of achieving the goal of living in a detached home. They were also claimed to be less expensive to furnish and cheaper to run than a conventional house. There were also bungalows with a bedroom or two in the roof, lit by a dormer window. Like the council house, the typical, privately built semi adopted a rectangular plan with a small kitchen, often called a 'kitchenette', within the main block. A serving hatch was another innovation of the time, linking the kitchen with the dining room, which usually had French windows opening on to the back garden. Occasionally the kitchen was located in a rear extension, but this was always of one floor. Generally the houses were low and wide and of just two storeys – the first floor containing three bedrooms and a bathroom, with the water closet often located in a separate room. Introduced from the United States in the late 1920s, coloured bathroom suites became popular in the 1930s, finished in a range of colours such as pink, green, primrose yellow and, for the avant-garde, black.

In 1925 Dudley was the first local authority to build council houses of cast-iron plates bolted together. The houses in Birmingham Road were of the non-parlour type, and the ironwork was locally made by the Eclipse Foundry Company. This pair is now preserved at the Black Country Living Museum.

The overriding style of the typical 1930s 'semi' was retrospective heavy borrowing from traditional vernacular motifs. Today it is frequently described as 'Tudorbethan' or 'Tudoresque' but at the time it was much derided by architectural critics. In 1938 Osbert Lancaster wrote of the 'Bypass Variegated' house and condemned the 'infernal amalgam' of past styles so commonly seen. The dominant feature was the front bay, usually

Derby Road, Liverpool. The typical environment of the privately built 1930s estate: wide grass verges separate the pavement from the road, whilst the planting of trees adds to the sense of semi-rural seclusion.

Metro Land: the Weller Estate at Woodside Close, Amersham, Buckinghamshire, built from 1930. On the left is a Type C house, a three-bedroom semi-detached with built-in garage, selling at £895; on the right is a Type B house with four bedrooms, on sale at £985.

Semi-bungalow with attic living space in Kellaway Avenue, Bristol, developed from the early 1920s.

A 1930s semi in Eastcote Road, Pinner, Middlesex. This pair has a single-storey rear extension accommodating the kitchen.

of two storeys, which was surmounted by a large prominent gable, typically dressed with bargeboards and fake timber framing in imitation of sixteenth- and seventeenth-century vernacular housing. The bays were variously square-edged or set at an angle (canted). Curved bays were also popular, either tucked under deep projecting eaves or surmounted by a projecting

1930s bungalows in Stanley Road, Hillingdon, Middlesex.

gable supported from below by open timber brackets. An oriel window was commonly used for the small third bedroom over the front door, whilst halls and landings were well lit by small, variously shaped windows on the ground floor – square, round or diamond – and by long vertical windows over the stairs. Breaking with some two hundred years of formal architectural practice, the sash window was abandoned in favour of casement windows with top-hung upper lights in stout timber frames. The casements were typically painted cream, contrasting with frames painted a darker colour such as mid-green or chocolate brown. There was another window in the front door: this was variously round, square, square with a wavy-arched top, or commonly a horizontal oval (with a drip rail above), and arranged over long vertical panels. There were usually long vertical glazed panels either side of the door, and the whole ensemble was commonly placed in a large, round-arched, open porch, and this, along with the timbered gable and bay window, forms one of the most recognisable stylistic components of a privately built 1930s house. Many of the windows were decorated with leaded lights and stained glass, which was usually combined with wavy or rippled glass. Much 1930s stained glass was in the modern style, relying on bold splashes of colour in geometric leadwork: a popular design consisted of long rays of contrasting coloured glass spreading outwards from a small 'rising sun' of red or yellow glass, although another widely found motif, which struck a more traditional note, was a Tudor galleon tossed on stormy seas. From the general run of the 'Tudorbethan'

The typical 1930s doorway in Westbury-on-Trym, Bristol. Within a brick, round-arched porch, the vertical-panelled door, painted mid-green, and the side lights contain modern-style glass.

Right: A rising sun design in stained glass, 1937.

Far right: Design for stained glass: a Tudor galleon tossed on stormy seas, 1932.

A 1930s two-storey bay given Gothic treatment – an embattled parapet and sash windows; Falcondale Road, Westbury-on-Trym, Bristol, c. 1935.

house, a few were given a pseudo-Gothic finish by substituting an embattled parapet for the usual gable. So there was extraordinary variety in privately built inter-war housing, not only from one development to the next, but very often in the same road, as builders deliberately widened the choice of houses available for sale. And yet, apart from the few houses finished in local stone, it is impossible to attribute any regional pattern to any of these styles.

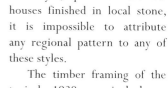

The timber framing of the typical 1930s semi had no structural function. Most houses were built of brick and, notwithstanding a few well-publicised exceptions, the quality of construction was excellent. This was the period when cavity wall construction became standard and walls were laid in stretcher bond with Portland cement in place of traditional lime mortar. But these were not glory days for the humble brick. The locally hand-made bricks that gave such character and charm to Georgian and Victorian houses were replaced by mass-produced bricks such as the harsh, pinkish Fletton. Large expanses of brick were frowned upon, so first floors were often rendered or covered in pebbledash – that is, pea shingle that was thrown against the final render coat. Alternatively, the shingle was mixed in with the render to create roughcast. Some houses were covered entirely in pebbledash, which looked arguably as harsh as the red brick underneath. However, brick could be used decoratively to help create the retrospective character of the 1930s house with brick nogging – that is, brick infill in a timber frame. Alternatively, the bays were clad in tile hanging, another vernacular tradition. The roofs were usually of hipped construction with red tiles, although glazed green tiles were sometimes used when walls were rendered white. Recalling the work of Voysey, some roof gables swept down to ground level with a mass of Tudor-style black and white timber framing to contain the porch.

While the typical inter-war middle-class house was smaller than its Edwardian and Victorian forebears, and its exterior styling often looked backwards, many aspects of the interior design reflected contemporary needs. Fewer middle-class families employed servants, so the house was designed to be labour-saving. Although the earliest council houses were usually lit by gas and built with solid-fuel ranges, virtually all privately built housing was supplied with electricity from new. Interior fittings such as the all-tiled

Appliqué timber framing, Southdown Road, Westbury-on-Trym, Bristol, c. 1935.

'Tudorbethan' vernacular: a first-floor oriel window set in brick nogging and timber framing under a half-timbered roof gable; Falcondale Road, Westbury-on-Trym, Bristol, c. 1935.

fireplaces and interior joinery were largely free of relief ornamentation that could harbour dust. Reflecting the rapid increase in car ownership in the 1930s, some houses were built with a garage to the side; typically, these had roofs and wooden doors with glazed upper panels that complemented the main façade.

The cosy semi-rural world of the Tudoresque villa was rudely shattered by a challenge from the aggressive, uncompromising

The typical unfitted 1930s kitchen, *Homes & Gardens*, May 1932.

Modern Movement. This was a European reaction to traditional styles which emerged in the 1920s, led by architects such as Le Corbusier (1887–1965), Walter Gropius (1883–1969) and Ludwig Mies van der Rohe (1886–1969). They rejected historical styles and any architectural decoration or whimsy. Ornament of any kind was to be banished as architecture searched for a purity and simplicity of design based on sheer functionalism. In achieving this, traditional building techniques were abandoned in favour of reinforced concrete, which enabled the architect to break all conventions of design. Cantilevered upper floors, large picture windows, flat roofs and the whole

A typical 1930s tiled fireplace with raised tiled hearth, 1932.

Suntrap house, Northwood Way, Northwood Hills, Middlesex, by Morgan and Edwards, 1934, with metal-framed windows – curved in the bay, white rendered walls and green roof tiles.

Private 1930s flats at Queens Court, Clifton, Bristol, built 1936–7; seventy-four luxury flats with underground parking.

Modern-style houses at Highover Park, Amersham, Buckinghamshire, by Amyas Connell and Basil Ward, c. 1934.

finished in stark white were the hallmarks of the movement. Some striking houses were built in the style – such as High and Over in Amersham, Buckinghamshire, designed by the New Zealand architect Amyas Connell (1901–80). Completed in 1929 and followed by four similar houses, High and Over received some critical acclaim from within the architectural profession but others complained of the overemphasis on function and its lack of artistic vocabulary. The Modern Movement never suited the British psyche – or the weather: it was seen as too impersonal, and large areas of glass were either too hot or too cold for the English climate. Nevertheless, a few middle-class apartment blocks around Greater

London were built in the Modern Style, and some elements were applied to houses of conventional construction. To John Betjeman, these were not 'modern', only 'jazz', with their flat, green-tiled roofs, white rendered walls and wide metal windows which curved around corners. These so-called 'suntrap' windows have given their name to this distinctive house type. The 'suntrap' house, however, never represented more than a minor footnote in the history of 1930s suburbia; it was always something of a curiosity, ultimately signifying the failure of the Modern Movement to win widespread acceptance before 1939.

Advertisement for steel-framed windows, *Homes & Gardens*, January 1938.

Modern-style private flats at Elm Park Court, Pinner, a development of seventy-seven apartments designed in 1934 by H. F. Webb.

POST-WAR HOUSING, 1945–75

ANOTHER WORLD WAR and another cessation in house-building brought another watershed in British house design. House-building slowed to a virtual standstill between 1939 and 1945. Through enemy action 475,000 houses had been destroyed or made uninhabitable, and slums remained a problem in many large towns and cities at the end of the war. In many towns and cities temporary accommodation was provided by prefabricated houses. Altogether 156,000 'prefabs' were assembled, using innovative materials such as steel and aluminium, and proved a successful and popular house type. Although many long outlived their life expectancy, prefabs were intended only as a temporary measure, and for the new post-war government the provision of new council housing was a top priority. Local authority house-building resumed in 1946, and of the 2.5 million new houses and flats built up to 1957, 75 per cent were local authority owned. The building of council houses in the post-war era was shaped by a new approach to town planning enshrined in the Greater London Plan of 1944, a blueprint for post-war reconstruction by Professor Patrick Abercrombie (1879–1957). Out of this came the idea of neighbourhood units and the new town movement, which revived the idea of the garden city, which had been lost in the building of the inter-war council estates. In 1945 a New Towns Committee created government-sponsored corporations which were given power to acquire land within a defined, designated area to establish new towns, and the New Towns Act, passed the following year, provided the government with the power to implement these plans. The result was the creation of twenty-two new towns between 1946 and 1972, many serving as satellite towns to Greater London. Stevenage was the first to be designated, followed by Crawley, Harlow and Hemel Hempstead in 1947. Later new towns included Skelmersdale (1961), Telford (1963) and Milton Keynes (1967).

The creation of new local authority estates and the new towns took place in a mood of optimism in which Modernist architects were given the opportunity to demonstrate that their rational, planned architecture would create a bright, new, Utopian world of clean, functional towns.

Opposite:
A Utopian dream in concrete. Tall blocks of flats with a range of facilities to make life pleasanter and easier, and 'clean-looking' individual houses – both built of reinforced concrete. From *Village and Town* by S. R. Badmin, 1942.

A Type B2
aluminium
prefabricated
bungalow from
Llandinam
Crescent, Gabalfa,
Cardiff, built
in 1948, and
re-erected at the
Museum of Welsh
Life, Cardiff.

Post-war house construction was also shaped by two housing reports: the Dudley Report of 1944, and the Parker Morris report, *Homes for Today and Tomorrow*, published in 1961. Property owning also rose sharply in the post-war era, growing from 26 per cent of all householders in England and Wales in 1945 to 49 per cent by 1970. In this period the difference in the standards of housing between professional and manual workers narrowed, and increasingly there was growing conformity between private and public house types in terms of space and amenities. Bungalows remained popular in the

The bathroom in a
Type 2 prefab at
the Museum of
Welsh Life.

private sector: they came to typify post-war suburbia in dormitory areas such as the Wirral and in many coastal developments. Stylistically, there were still differences between public and privately built houses. Inevitably, greater variety of styles and types of dwelling were to be found in private developments, and houses of the 1950s and 1960s are now beginning to acquire a period character of their own.

The post-war estate layout was founded on the principle of the 'neighbourhood unit', a planning concept that promoted the development of self-contained communities. As a reaction to the social homogeneity and physical monotony of the typical pre-war council estate, the neighbourhood unit was intended to incorporate a wider social mix and a greater variety of house types. It was hoped that the neighbourhood units would foster, as Bristol's 1952 Development Plan explained, 'a co-operative spirit between the social classes … to overcome the social and civic difficulties from which the large city suffers'. Some neighbourhood units were built 'phoenix-like' out of the slums they replaced as part of urban regeneration schemes, whilst others – like many pre-war council estates – were built on new green-field sites on the edges of towns.

A greater variety of house types typified the neighbourhood unit and included blocks and flats as well as three-bedroom semi-detached houses. Some houses were of conventional brick construction, but, to reduce building costs, others were made of non-traditional materials, such as precast reinforced concrete. These houses were available as proprietary brands, such

Design for a block of flats by Liverpool City Council, December 1945. Drawing by Fred Jenkins (1888–1955).

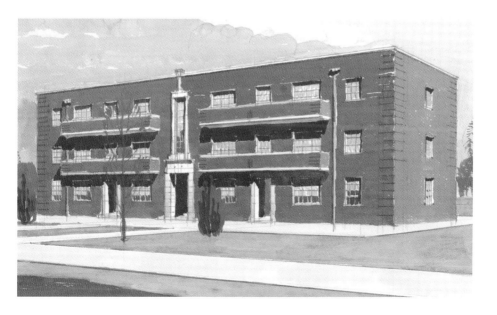

Three rows of back-to-backs in Leeds, seen before demolition in an undated photograph of *c*. 1960. The nearest house is 111 Freehold Street, which lay back-to-back with 109, which was at the front of the street. Council houses in Glenthorpe Crescent, built on former allotments, are seen in the left background.

as the 'Cornish', 'Unity', 'Woolaway' and 'Reema', developed and marketed by different builders, and they generally relied upon concrete panels reinforced with steel and either bolted together or held by a steel frame. The design of the houses was generally plainer and simpler, and roofs were pitched lower. Following the recommendations contained in the Dudley Report, post-war council houses were provided with more space and better services, including better storage facilities. In some of the new towns and council estates built in the 1950s a new type of house layout known as the 'Radburn', which aimed to separate vehicular and pedestrian access, was introduced. The orthodox street frontage was abandoned in favour of the use of road access by cul-de-sacs, with access to the front door by a pedestrian footpath across a small open grassed area, with no obvious boundaries between individual properties.

The traditional 'semi' went into decline during the 1950s and the number of flats and maisonettes built by local authorities increased. Blocks of flats or maisonettes were invariably flat-roofed and either low – often being four storeys high in a variety of shapes, such as T-blocks, Y-blocks and cruciform blocks – or 'point blocks', that is tall buildings standing apart from their surroundings. The first high-rise block was the ten-storey The Lawn at Harlow, Essex, designed by Frederick Gibberd (1908–84) and completed

'Easyform' two-storey flats of concrete, cast on site, built in Hungerford Road on the Stockwood Estate, Bristol. From the mid-1950s 824 acres of agricultural land were developed to rehouse residents of condemned inner-city slums.

in 1951. The building of blocks of five or more storeys accounted for just 9 per cent of local authority building between 1953 and 1959 but increased in the early 1960s to reach a peak of 26 per cent in 1966. High-rise flats represented an architectural ideal for architects and planners who had come under the influence of the Modern Movement and pioneers such as Le Corbusier and Walter Gropius in the 1930s. The high-density, vertical city was to replace the outward expansion of the conventional city, which threatened the surrounding countryside. By the mid-1950s it was government policy to extend green belt nationwide and there was a new

'Cornish' units on the Horfield Estate, Bristol, 1950s.

subsidy arrangement by which for the first time grants increased with blocks of more than six storeys, leading to the adoption of tall point blocks of up to twenty-two storeys in Sheffield and Salford. In Glasgow and London some exceeded thirty storeys: Trellick Tower, North Kensington, designed by Ernő Goldfinger (1902–87) and completed in 1972, has thirty-one storeys containing 217 flats, and is 98 metres tall.

Another key aspect of the tower-block vision was the 'Brutalist' style of architecture. The name came from the French *beton brut* ('raw concrete') and was coined by the British architects Alison (1928–93) and Peter (1923–2003) Smithson in 1954. The Brutalists favoured stark and striking tower blocks with large sections of exposed concrete. Concrete was an integral part of the tower-block design. It offered boundless flexibility to the building designers; it was economical – it could be poured on site – and, moreover, it was believed to be long-lasting, if not indestructible. Brutalist architecture relied for its visual impact on sheer mass and large expanses of rough, grey concrete. Structural 'honesty' and functionalism, in line with Le Corbusier's original philosophy of the 1920s, guided the Brutalist architects. Where decoration was found, it usually consisted of sections of wall filled with abstract designs in tiles, random stonework or coloured plastics, but the

The Brutalist concrete, brick and glass panorama of Park Hill, Sheffield, built in 1961 to a design by Ivor Smith and Jack Lynn.

overall visual effect of a typical block was created by the seemingly endless repetition of the individual dwelling marked by the large picture windows and shallow balconies. Some towers were linked by flying corridors to service blocks containing laundries or, as at Trellick Tower, to a separate full-height tower containing the lifts and services.

Cumbernauld, a new town in Lanarkshire begun in 1955, was built as a Corbusian concrete Utopia, and Park Hill, a massive Brutalist concrete structure built on a hill overlooking the centre of Sheffield, was intended to signal the rejuvenation of the city and provide quality homes in a deprived area. Built in 1961, Park Hill was designed by two young Modernist architects, Ivor Smith and Jack Lynn. It consisted of huge snake-like blocks containing 995 dwellings, housing over two thousand people. The front door of each apartment opened on to a 12-foot-wide access deck, or 'street', which ran from one side of the complex to the other. Bridges carried the street through the entire scheme, enabling milk floats to pass from door to door. The architects were keen to preserve a sense of community and, as the lobby space in other Modernist blocks tended to become a no man's land, neither serving public needs nor offering privacy to residents, it was hoped that the 'streets' would solve this problem while preserving something of the

Waring House, Redcliffe, Bristol, c. 1960. This huge L-shaped block of council maisonettes and flats was completed in 1960.

atmosphere of traditional street life. So that the residents' individuality would not be smothered by the gargantuan surroundings, different-coloured linoleum was laid at each doorstep. But attempts to create a sense of community within the bleak concrete environment of large blocks failed, and developments such as Cumbernauld new town and Park Hill came to be almost universally loathed. Mounting criticism of their social and visual shortcomings and the structural failure of Ronan Point, a twenty-three-storey prefabricated concrete tower block in Newham, London, in 1968 caused a strong reaction against the building of more high-rise blocks. After 1970 the concrete tower block was no longer seen as a workable model for urban regeneration, although several blocks, including The Lawn, Trellick Tower and the Park Hill complex, have been given listed status by English Heritage.

The Parker Morris report of 1961 recommended standards for all new homes, public and private, which reflected changing patterns of living with more informality in the way space in the house was used. The main recommendations were for more living and circulation space and better

Design for a fitted kitchen with stainless steel sink, 1954.

heating throughout the house, so that all spaces could be used freely. The idea of a parlour set aside for best was abandoned in favour of two living spaces, one for private or quiet activity and the other for eating, although the latter could be part of an enlarged kitchen. The kitchen was to be extensively fitted and provided with plenty of space for storage and the use of electric domestic appliances, such as washing machines and refrigerators. These recommendations were made mandatory for public-sector housing in 1967 and briefly for local-authority housing in 1969 and, although they were never made mandatory for private housing, their influence was widely felt.

In the private sector there was a marked trend towards a growth in the size of operations, with large building firms such as Taylor Woodrow, Laing and Wimpey using architects to bring high standards of construction and design to the privately built post-war house. Typical features of the plan included garages linked or integrated with the main house; covered but open-fronted parking spaces were marketed as 'car ports'. Some halls were spacious and well lit with low horizontal or long vertical windows, and overlooked by 'gallery' landings. Other features of the interior included L-shaped open living areas with space for a dining area at one end and opening through French windows to a paved sitting-out area, the 'patio'; a downstairs water closet or small 'study' was often incorporated in the ground-floor plan. In keeping with the Parker Morris report, some kitchens contained a dining space so that they became family rooms, whilst there was much emphasis on the luxury fitted kitchen with a stainless steel sink and work-tops.

Exterior styling varied but there were, nevertheless, common characteristics that give 1960s housing an identity of its own. Plain, flat wall surfaces with large oblong 'picture' windows were typical. The windows usually had robust wooden frames with opening top lights. Front doors were usually glazed in small panels, often with rippled or reeded glass, while the woodwork was painted a light colour: white, pale blue and primrose yellow were popular. Some roofs were flat, but the typical 1960s house has a low-pitched roof with an end gable finished with a prominent but unadorned bargeboard, painted white. Roof tiles were generally of brown or grey concrete and, although red-brick walls were found on 1960s housing, light brown, grey or buff-coloured bricks were widely favoured. Claddings of tiles (usually of concrete) or white-painted clapboard applied between the ground- and first-floor windows were typical of the 1960s house and continued to be popular into the 1970s. The external design of some houses took its inspiration from Scandinavian models and these are instantly recognisable for their steeply pitched roofs, gable to the front, filled with vertical timbers and sweeping almost to the ground. The same

Block of private
flats faced in white
weatherboarding
and brown
brickwork on the
corner of Well
Lane and Kings
Road, Higher
Bebington, which
were built c. 1971
on the site of a
large detached
Victorian house.

effect was often continued inside, with pine-panelled kitchens and
timbered ceilings. Also popular in the 1960s were neo-Georgian style
houses characterised by red-brick walls, pedimented porches, small-paned
windows and fake louvred shutters. A larger style, sometimes called
'Colonial', had double garages under a colonnaded façade incorporating
bow windows and concrete urns.

For the first time in five hundred years the roof line of many new houses
was unbroken by chimney stacks. From the early 1960s, following the
recommendations of the Parker Morris report, most new houses were built
with full or partial central heating; moreover, the use of open coal fires had
declined since the passing of the Clean Air Act in 1956. Some houses retained
an open fireplace as a feature, with a prominent end-gable flue, sometimes
built – or at least clad – in stone to add 'character' to the house, whilst in the
living room the fireplace opening was surrounded in stonework. In the later
1960s 'Cotswold' stone fireplaces became popular, regardless of the
underlying local geology. The grate often contained a back boiler capable of
heating two or three radiators and a towel rail, although after 1960 oil and
gas central heating systems were widely adopted and the fireplace – if there
was one – was more likely to be filled with an electric 'log-effect' fire.
Between 1971 and 1983 the number of homes with central heating almost

doubled from 34 per cent to 64 per cent. Comfort, convenience and efficiency – in the utilisation of space and the consumption of energy – were now established as the chief factors shaping the future of urban house design.

Between 1945 and 1982 some four million privately built houses were added to the housing stock. They are to be found everywhere but typically are seen on the edges of towns in new developments, often preserving elements of the garden city ideal with estates of small three-bedroom houses fronted by open lawns in small winding roads and cul-de-sacs. Town and city centres, meanwhile, declined as areas of older housing were cleared. The impulse was outwards to the suburbs and to new dormitory towns that swallowed up small villages and farmsteads – places such as Yate and Nailsea, near Bristol. As a consequence, by the 1970s towns and cities were larger than their Victorian predecessors but less densely populated. After 1975 new house-building in both the public and private sectors declined. This and other changes marked the end of the post-war era in town housing and also the end of an era in urban domestic architecture. The optimism of the 1950s and early 1960s for the new council developments faded. The building of tower blocks ceased. The Housing Act of 1980 gave five million council-house tenants the right to buy their home from the local authority, and the number

Detached semi-bungalow in Well Lane, Higher Bebington, with 'feature' stone chimney, built around 1967.

Semi-detached houses on the privately developed Elm House Estate, Tee Hay Road, Higher Bebington, Wirral, built c. 1961, with oil central heating and car ports but no chimneys. The near house appears to retain the original wooden windows.

of council-owned houses soon fell. The era of the building of large council estates was over, and the responsibility for the development and provision of social housing – that is, 'affordable' housing let at low rents and on a secure basis to people in need – moved increasingly to housing associations. This had its own impact on architecture as the new owner-occupiers of former council houses sought to stamp their own personality on their house with new porches, extensions and stone cladding; thus the uniformity of the council estates began to disintegrate. In the private sector there was a revival, too, from the mid-1970s of the vernacular tradition, as a reaction set in against Modernism and contemporary style.

This short history of town house architecture began with the arrival of classical architecture in the mid-seventeenth century. It ends in the 1970s with a reaffirmation of the vernacular tradition. In the mid-twentieth century supporters of the Modern Movement, such as Frederick Gibberd, wrote of the inevitability of the rise of that movement. It was presented as an all-embracing architectural code, just as classicism had provided a new aesthetic in the 1640s. Modernism promised a new dawn. It was free of the assumptions that had shackled traditional architecture and could answer society's demand for good housing with architecture that was honest and functional. Therefore, it was right. To oppose Modernism was to reject the inevitability of progress. But in rejecting all that had gone before the Modernists lost the understanding accrued over centuries of how houses function and how people wish to live their everyday lives. So they never achieved widespread popular support. The construction of high-rise estates in the first half of the 1960s created new environments where old social problems such as crime and vandalism thrived, but also caused some to lament the passing of the old Victorian townscapes. Critical opinion had turned a full circle. Those gridiron streets of Victorian by-law housing were now valued for their human scale, for their sense of community with their corner pubs and shops, and also for their character.

Into the twenty-first century new trends are evident but, as we move closer to our own time, historical perspective blurs and breaks down. Modernism is not dead – it lives on now as just one of several design options; it is particularly favoured for the large apartment blocks to be found in dockland regeneration schemes. Social housing is characteristically low-rise, small-scale and simply finished. In the private sector large housing companies continue to build in a range of traditional styles, often striving to complement local traditions and building types, albeit combined with white plastic double-glazed windows. Mock timber framing is back, so are steeper-pitched roofs, dormers, gables and bay windows, echoing late-Victorian town architecture, and confirming the enduring appeal of Britain's architectural heritage stretching back more than three hundred years.

FURTHER READING

Ayres, James. *Building the Georgian City*. Yale, New Haven and London, 1998.

Betjeman, John. *English Cities and Small Towns*. Collins, 1943.

Bradbury, Oliver C. *Cheltenham's Lost Heritage*. Sutton, Stroud, 2004.

Brunskill, R. W. *Illustrated Handbook of Vernacular Architecture*. Faber & Faber, 1971.

Burnett, John. *A Social History of Housing*. David & Charles, Newton Abbot, 1978.

Burton, Neil, and Chadwick, Dan. *Life in the Georgian City*. Viking Press, London, 1990.

Campbell, Colen. *Vitruvius Britannicus*. 1715, 1717 and 1725; Dover Publications, Mineola, New York, 2007.

Guillery, Peter. *The Small House in Eighteenth Century London*. Yale University Press, New Haven and London, 2004.

Ison, Walter. *The Georgian Buildings of Bath*. Faber, London, 1948.

Ison, Walter. *The Georgian Buildings of Bristol*. Kingsmead, 1952.

Jackson, Alan A. *London's Metroland*. Capital History, 2006.

Lancaster, Osbert. *From Pillar to Post*. John Murray, London, 1938.

Loudon, John Claudius. *Cottage, Farm and Villa Architecture*. Longman, London, 1833.

Millais, Malcolm. *Exploding the Myths of Modern Architecture*. Frances Lincoln, London, 2009.

Muthesius, Hermann. *Das Englische Haus*. Berlin, 1904–5. (The English House, Granada, London, 1979.)

Muthesius, Stefan. *The English Terraced House*. Yale, New Haven and London, 1982.

Nicholson, P. *The New Practical Builder and Workman's Companion*. Thomas Kelly, London, 1823.

Pevsner, Nikolaus. *Buildings of England* series. Penguin, Harmondsworth, from 1951.

Rock, Alistair. *The 1930s House Manual*. Haynes, Yeovil, 2005.

Summerson, John. *Georgian London*. Pleiades, London, 1945.

Thom, Colin. *Researching London's Houses*. Historical Publications, 2005.

Upton, Chris. *Living Back-to-Back*. Phillimore, Chichester, 2005.

Wedd, Kitt. *The Victorian House*. Aurum Press, London, 2002.

INDEX

FORTY M

PUB WA
IN DORSET

Forty Circular Walks

Around Dorset Inns

Mike Power

Other local publications available

Pub Walks in Dorset
Pub Walks in Hampshire & I.O.W.
The Dorset Coast Path
Along Longham

1st Edition Published June 1991

© **M. Power 1991**

ISBN 0 9514 502 4 7

Publisher's Note

Whilst every care has been taken to ensure the accuracy of all the information given in this book at the time of printing, errors will occur due to many factors. Paths are sometimes re-routed, new stiles replace old gates or wooden crossing points. The pubs themselves regularly change hands which usually means a change of beer and menu. Also the inevitable printing error. Neither the printers nor the publishers can accept responsibility for any inaccuracies.

Power Publications
1, Clayford Avenue, Ferndown,
Dorset BH22 9PQ

Printed by Pardy Printers Ltd, Ringwood, Hants.

Front cover: The Bottle Inn, Marshwood

INTRODUCTION

During the research for my first book, *Pub Walks in Dorset*, I visited numerous inns throughout Dorset and discovered many enjoyable walks. The problem came when I had to select just forty; it meant that some very good pubs were not included, also some very enjoyable walks had to be omitted. Thanks to the success of that book, and popular demand for more walks, it has enabled me to now include them in this second book.

As with the first book this one too covers the whole county from Birdsmoorgate in the west, Stour Provost in the north and Tuckton in the east. The walks vary in length from $2\frac{1}{4}$ miles to $6\frac{3}{4}$ miles with the average being between $3\frac{1}{2}$ and 5 miles. I have avoided giving the approximate time any particular walk is likely to take; we all walk at a different pace and conditions can vary greatly. But, for those who would like some idea, you should allow for two miles per hour.

As all the walks are planned to start and finish at a pub it is assumed you would wish to partake of their hospitality. But on the odd occasion you do not, or if you think you might not make it back before closing time, and in fairness to the licensees, I would respectfully ask you not to use their own car parks. Where possible we have indicated suitable alternative parking areas.

The new 'Rights of Way' Act, which came into force on August 13th, 1990, has much improved the rights of ramblers; it is a massive step forward in path protection. The Act now requires occupiers who disturb the land to make good the surface within 24 hours of the disturbance or two weeks if the disturbance is the first one for a particular crop. Where no width is recorded the minimum width of a path must be one metre and two metres for a bridleway and the exact line of the path must be apparent on the ground. Furthermore the occupier must prevent crops growing on, or encroaching onto the path. You should report any problems you find to the relevant authority.

Any person using a public footpath has the right to remove as much of the obstruction as necessary to allow him or her to pass, but not to cause wilful damage to property. If the obstruction cannot be removed the walker is entitled to leave the path and walk round it, causing no more damage than is necessary. If the path has been sown with crops you are entitled to follow the route even if it means treading on the crops.

The new definitive map for Dorset was published on the 29th September, 1989, and shows all the claimed legal routes of the footpaths, bridleways and byways within the county. Copies are available for inspection at the County, District and Parish Council Offices and also at all main libraries. There are two Ordnance Survey Maps to help locate the paths; the Landranger series 1:50 000, $1\frac{1}{4}$ inch to one mile or the more detailed Pathfinder 1:25 000, $2\frac{1}{2}$ inch to 1 mile. It is always advisable to have a map with you. The marking of public footpaths is being improved all the time but it will still be a while before they are all completed.

Wherever you go, always follow the country code. Fasten all gates. Keep dogs under control and always on a lead where there are livestock. Take your litter home. Do not pick wild flowers or dig up the plants and remember to keep to the right-hand side of the road where there are no pavements.

I very much enjoyed writing this second book, I hope you too will enjoy it.

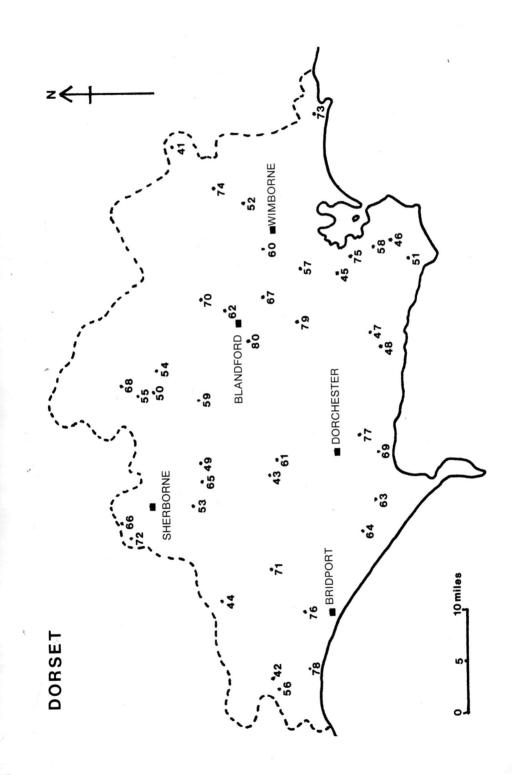

DORSET

N

WIMBORNE

BLANDFORD

SHERBORNE

DORCHESTER

BRIDPORT

0   5   10 miles

The Churchill Arms, Alderholt

The Churchill Arms is a popular village local. From the front entrance porch two bars lead off on either side both similarly and comfortably furnished. The walls are panelled in a light brown coloured wood. One bar has a close boarded white painted ceiling with a small attractive fireplace. Leading off to the back is another bar with a pool table. There is also a separate function room, a skittle alley and a children's room. At the back is a secluded beer garden with play area.

It is a Hall & Woodhouse pub with two real ales: Badger Best and Eagle Bitter.

Food can be chosen from the set menu or from the daily specials board in the bar. Of the various bar snacks jacket potatoes feature strongly with some ten different fillings. There are also various salads, sandwiches cut to order, both plain and toasted, ploughman's and a picnic plate—stilton or cheddar, pickles, salad, beetroot, sausage, ham and roll and butter. Main meals include chicken, haddock, seafood platter, steak, gammon and home-made steak and kidney pie. There is a roast lunch on Sunday and a separate children's menu. The specials board usually offers a starter such as home-made French onion soup, a choice of main courses and home-made sweets such as rhubarb crumble.

Families are welcome but dogs are not allowed.

Weekday opening hours are from 11 a.m. till 2.30 p.m. and 6 p.m. till 11 p.m.

Telephone: (0425) 652147.

The pub is in the centre of the village on the Cranborne to Fordingbridge road.

Approx. distance of walk: 4 miles. O.S. Map 195 SU 114/125.

Park in the inn's own car park or at the start of the walk in Blackwater Grove.

A most enjoyable walk on bridleways, across farm land, and through woods. It is an easy walk for families at any time of the year but can be a bit muddy in the winter. One of the best times is mid to late March when the wild daffodils are out. The sheer number in bloom along the track north from the church is one of the best displays I have seen on any walk.

Leave the inn and turn left, cross the road and turn right into Blackwater Grove. Walk down to the bottom and on to the forest track. When you reach the fence by the farm buildings, turn right, go over the stile beside the gate and turn left. Before reaching the corner of the field cut across to the stile on the right, go over the disused railway track, through the gate and bear left, following the path around the enclosed field until you reach a signed footpath into the wood.

Cross the drive and continue straight ahead bearing left by the double gates then follow the path over the crossing point into the woods, it is well signed and easy to follow. Cross over the bridge and turn left walking up the wide grass track to the road. Go straight across and up the tarred track to the stile, it is signed Bullhill ¾. Continue

ahead, keeping close to the hedge on the right, over another stile, up to the corner of the field then turn left. On the right is a stile beside a gate leading on to a long wide track. In spring there are masses of wild daffodils all along the way.

Go out into the lane and bear right. It is a quiet peaceful lane with very little traffic. After about ¾ of a mile look for a stile in the hedge on the right. Go over, and bear left, down the field to the stile by the stream. Cross over and head up the field, bearing slightly left, to the side of the house, go out through the gate, on to the track and turn right. Ignore any side turnings just keep to the main track, through a couple of gates, until you eventually reach the road then turn left back to the pub.

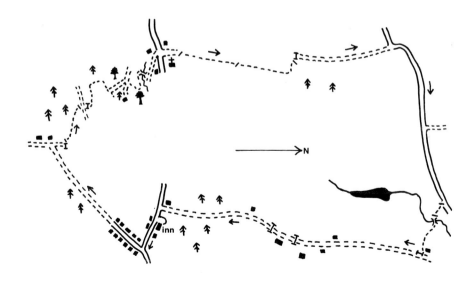

The sketch maps in this book are not necessarily to scale but have been drawn to show the maximum amount of detail.

Rose & Crown Inn, Birdsmoorgate

In 1856 Birdsmoorgate was thrust into the public gaze. Martha Brown, who ran a shop locally, found her much younger husband sitting on the knee of Mary Powell who also ran a shop in the village. That night when she returned home she attacked and killed him with an axe. The inquest was held in The Rose and Crown, and after being found guilty at her trial in Dorchester, she became the last person to be publicly hanged in Dorset. Thomas Hardy, who at the age of 16 witnessed the execution, was probably influenced by what he saw when he wrote Tess of the D'Urbervilles. Tess, like Martha, ended her life on the scaffold.

Records show that The Rose & Crown has been a pub for the last 300 years. This two storey inn occupies a high position in this beautiful part of rural Dorset. There are two bars and a separate dining room which doubles as a games room in the winter. The rustic style interior is simply furnished with chairs and bench seating. Outside there is a children's play area and beer garden. It is a freehouse well run by the friendly owners, Stan, Stella and Lynne Cornock.

There is usually a choice of four real ales. Two from Eldridge Pope: Thomas Hardy Bitter, and the stronger Royal Oak, Wadsworth 6X plus a guest beer.

From the menu you have a choice of bar snacks which include generous ploughman's, sandwiches and toasties. Several home-made dishes include reasonably priced steak and kidney, 'Old Peculiar' casserole and often a lamb hot pot. Steak come in all sizes including a genuine '24 ouncer'. One popular dish is swordfish steak.

Opening hours can be flexible but as a rule the inn opens at 10 a.m. till 2.30 p.m. and again from 6 p.m. till 11 p.m.

Children are welcome.

Telephone: (02977) 527.

The pub is situated north from Morcombelake on the crossroads where the B3165 meets the B3164.

Approx. distance of walk: 4¾ miles. O.S. Map No. 195 SY 392/009.

There is ample parking behind and to the side of the pub. Some people also park by the small green opposite.

A most enjoyable 'snowdrop walk'. At first along the banks of the river Synderford to Saddle Street and through the peaceful village of Thorncombe. It then takes you across farmland down to Sadborrow, and finally back across Payne's Down. It is a delightful walk at any time of the year but to appreciate the masses of snowdrops and wild daffodils along the river bank the best time is March, provided you can cope with the mud!

Turn left from the inn walking down until you reach the bend in the road, You will see a short track off to the left. Turn down here, go through the farm gate and along the track. Most people I would imagine keep to the track but it seems from the definitive map that the footpath possibly diverts through the gate on the left, skirts the hedge for a short distance before returning to the track across the little bridge. Continue following the track, over a cattle grid and up a concrete drive until you reach the gate on the left. Go through following the path close to the course of the river. In early spring it is an absolute picture when both river banks are covered in swathes of snowdrops inter

spersed with primroses and wild daffodils.

Keeping close to the river bank, continue ahead, through a gate, into a small copse, out through another gate, over a rough track and straight ahead over a pair of stiles. Further on another stile takes you into a small attractive wood. Follow the path through, crossing the small tributary as best you can, then over the stile and into the field ahead. After crossing another small tributary keep straight ahead to the stile. Continue through a couple more gates until you enter a small thicket. Go through it and over the wooden crossing point still following the river until you reach a wooden crossing point and a bridge on the left.

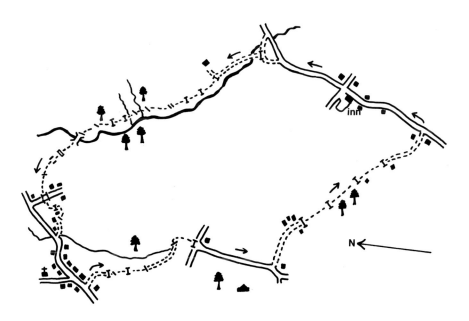

9

Cross over into the field and bear right to a wooden crossing point. Continue straight ahead, through a rather boggy area to a gap in the hedge opposite. If it is very wet you will find it easier to make a wide sweep up the bank.

Go into the field, and bear right, heading up to meet the hedge then continue walking, into the field ahead and up round to the gate in the top corner.

Cross the road, go through the gate opposite, keep straight ahead then go through the gate in the hedge on the left. Turn right walking behind the farm buildings, through into the field ahead and immediately over the stile on the right opposite the cottages. Turn left walking down the drive and over the ford into the lane. Turn left up the hill to Thorncombe. After passing the post office look for a track on the left; it is not signed but it runs down between a couple of houses. After a short distance it merges with a

narrow track before reaching a gate. Go through into the field and over the stile. In the winter it can become very muddy. Continue ahead, keeping fairly close to the hedge on the left, through the gate and across the field to the stile. Follow the path along the edge of the wooded ravine until you eventually reach a stile on the left. Go into the field, turn right and leave by the gate in the far hedge.

Walk straight across the road and down the lane to Sadborow. Turn left when you reach the drive to Grighay Farm. Continue ahead, between the farm buildings and through the gate into the field. Make your way across to the gate in the far hedge and continue ahead keeping close to the wood on the right. Go through another gate and finally through one last gate by the house. Follow the track up to the road and turn left back to the pub.

The Cerne Giant

Royal Oak, Cerne Abbas

If I go hill walking at Cerne on a cold winters day there is nothing I like more than to end up in The Royal Oak with a pint of well kept real ale, a bowl of their tasty home-made soup and warm myself in front of one of their open fires. This attractive 16th-century inn was built, it is said, partly out of stone from the ruined Benedicton Abbey around the time of the Reformation in 1540. In 1771 the inn changed hands for five shillings. In its time it has been a blacksmith's shop and an old coaching stop. There are three communicating rooms each with its own charm. One has a boarded ceiling the others are beamed. Two of the rooms are heated by open fires. Seating is provided by an assortment of wooden settles, cosy high back benches and farmhouse chairs. The area around the servery still displays the magnificent flag stone floor. The inn is beautifully kept, the many copper and brass items on display all positively gleam with loving care and attention. An interesting display of cups hang from the beams. Outside is a terrace with picnic benches. I last visited the inn at Christmas. The decorations were magnificent; the best I have ever seen anywhere so I was not surprised to learn that it takes three days to put them all up.

It is a Devenish House offering three real ales: Devenish JD, Royal Wessex and Marston's Pedigree.

Good home cooked food is available seven days a week. You can have a snack such as a ploughman's lunch or sandwiches, or choose from the set menu which includes steaks, omelettes, home-cooked ham and steak and kidney pie. Each day a blackboard lists several specials. They can include home-made chicken and vegetable curry, smoked salmon, lasagne and fried brie with cranberry sauce.

The inn is open from 11 a.m. till 2.30 p.m. and 6 p.m. till 11 p.m.

Telephone: (0300) 341270.

Village situated north of Dorchester on the A352.

Approx. distance of walk: 6 miles. O.S. Map No. 184 ST 665/013

You can park safely almost anywhere in the village.

A fairly long but most enjoyable scenic walk, a little demanding in places especially in winter when the steep path to the top of Giant Hill can become a bit slippery. The route back takes you through the hamlets of Minterne Parva and through Cerne park where you have a good view of the 180 foot high Cerne Giant.

Leave the inn and turn left on the Buckland Newton road. After passing the last house go through the little gate on the left and bear right across the field to the stile opposite. Continue in the same direction to the stile in the far top corner, go out onto the track and turn left. Although the bridleway is raised it does become very muddy in the winter and during wet weather. At the top of the hill go through the gate then immediately left through the smaller gate. Turn right through the gate by the barn and, keeping to the path beside the hedge, continue ahead until you reach the small gate on the left. Walk down and across the field, bearing slightly right, through the gate at the bottom and turn right. After a few steps head left, down the hillside to the gate at the bottom.

The well worn path crosses the field to meet a track at the bottom which joins with a similar track in the centre of Minterne Parva. Turn left and keep walking until you reach the A352. Turn left again and then right on the road to Up Cerne. You have only a short distance to walk along the main

road but as it is round a right-hand bend it is probably safer to keep to the left-hand side of the road.

Continue through the village past the Manor House until you reach the bend in the road and go up the track on the right. After passing the small wood you come to a signed bridleway on the left. Follow the track until it bears left beside a field. At this point go into the field and straight across, through the hedge opposite, onto the bridleway and turn left. Just before reaching the radio mast go into the field on the left and across, making for the corner of the wood. Bear right, and go through the gap into the woods taking the right fork to the bottom.

Cross into the field ahead. There is a small stile beside the gate. Continue down the field to the stile at the bottom, straight ahead, over another stile following the track through two more gates to meet a wide track from the left. Turn right and right again when you reach the main road. Walk past the viewing point for the giant and left down to the village, turning left when you reach the centre.

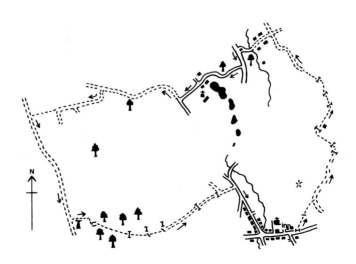

Winyards Gap Inn, Chedington

This ancient inn occupies a unique site close to the Somerset border overlooking the Axe Valley. The pub has been mentioned over the years in the works of several well known authors; among them Thomas Hardy who referred to the inn in his poem 'A Trampwoman's Tragedy'. In 1837 it was called the King's Arms but by the census of 1841 had become The Winyards Gap Inn. The warm friendly atmosphere of this lovely pub is apparent from the moment you walk through the front door. The cosy, beamed interior is comfortably furnished and carpeted throughout. Plain walls are adorned with a wealth of brightly shining old artifacts. At one end is an attractive warm wood burning stove on a raised hearth. There is a separate cosy dining room with high backed wooden settles, another bar to the right of the main entrance, a sunny front terrace and a large lawn beer garden.

The inn is a freehouse offering a good choice of drinks which includes mulled wine in the winter. There are usually three real ales plus a guest beer such as Ringwood Fortyniner, Exmoor Ale and Flowers Original.

The food is excellent, all meals cooked to order and available seven days a week including Sunday evening. Light meals offer a choice of home-made soup, ploughman's, filled jacket potatoes, kedgeree and 'the Landlord's favourite' smoked salmon, scrambled eggs and salad garnish. A speciality is the inn's own individually cooked pies. The 'Publican's special' uses best braised steak with oysters, cooked with Guinness. 'Dorset Cream Chicken' is generous pieces of chicken in a creamy sherry sauce with mushrooms and peppers served on a bed of rice. There is also a separate children's menu. If you still have an appetite and are not on a diet try one of their delicious traditional puddings, spotted dick or jam roly poly.

Accommodation is available in two delightful self-catering flats in a barn conversion next to the inn.

Opening times can be flexible but as a rule are from 11.30 a.m. till 3 p.m. and 7 p.m. till 11 p.m.

Telephone: (0935) 891244.

13

Walk No. 44

The Pub is on the A356, 15 miles north from Dorchester close to the border with Somerset.

Approx. distance of walk: 4¾ miles. O.S. Map. 194 ST 492/062.

There is a large car park beside the pub, also a small lay-by further down the lane towards Chedington.

A favourite walk of mine in this lovely scenic part of West Dorset. It takes you through the peaceful historic village of Chedington and the tiny hamlet of Weston. The walk is on farm land, bridleways and quiet country lanes. Although hilly the going is fairly easy but it does become a bit muddy in the winter.

Leave the inn and turn left. If you want to visit the monument to the 43rd Wessex division go up the steps by the lay-by. Continue along the lane to Chedington. This delightful village has some 17th and 18th-century houses. At the end of the village the road bears left to meet the lane at the top. Walk straight across and down the track to

Broadleaze Farm. When you reach the farm, you will see a small wooden crossing point on the left. Go into the field and down behind the farm buildings leaving by the small wooden gate in the fence at the bottom. The path through the small band of trees is not very clear. If you first bear left, before walking down to the trees you will

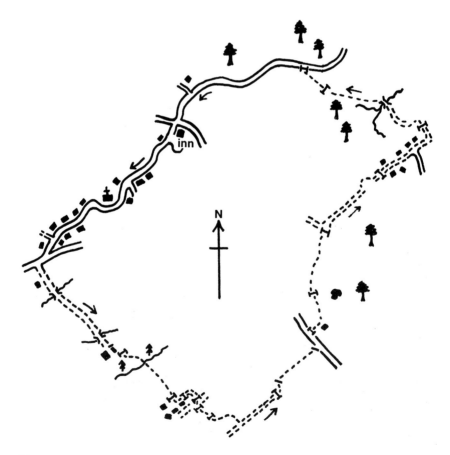

find a narrow gap. Walk down to the stream, across and through what remains of a gateway then straight up the field ahead towards the farm.

At the top go through the gate and turn left, out through the gate at the end of the farmyard and follow the track round, through another gate, across the track and through a similar gate on to a narrow strip of grass enclosed by wire fencing. Continue up through another gate into the field and bear left up to a gap in the hedge. Go through and straight across leaving the field by a gap in the hedge opposite, onto a grass track and turn left. Some distance ahead you reach a small gate, go through and bear left, round round the field, over the stile in the hedge and turn right. Keeping close to the hedge, walk up to the top of the field, over the stile, out into the road and turn left.

Carefully cross over to the other side. After a short walk you will come to a pair of farm gates. Go through them and straight ahead bearing left at the farm building. Walk down between the gate posts follow-

ing the track to the bottom, taking time as you go to admire the glorious view. Continue ahead through the wooden gate, down into the field, keeping to the well defined track close to the hedge on the left. At the bottom go through the farm gate and straight ahead towards Weston.

As you approach the first house the footpath has been diverted left on to a grass track behind the out buildings, it is signed. Rejoin the track and continue ahead through the gate, past more houses and farm buildings, until the track ends abruptly in front of a field gate. At this point turn left walking beside the wire fence then go through the gate ahead of you into the field. Turn left and walk round, keeping fairly close to the hedge on the left, down the track and across the stream at the bottom. Go up the field ahead keeping to a line close to the hedge on the right. In the far top corner of the field there is a farm gate. Go through and continue ahead up towards Crook Hill. Go out through the gate at the top, into the lane, and turn left back to the pub.

Cheddington Village

The Silent Woman, Coldharbour

This remote inn, surrounded by forest, was originally a farmhouse part of which dates back to the 18th-century. It was originally named the Angel and is referred to in Thomas Hardy's book 'The Return Of The Native'. The Silent Woman refers to a beheaded saint. Although other stories tell of a previous landlady who talked too much. Local smugglers fearing she might give away their secrets cut out the woman's tongue. The inn has been altered and added to over the years but still retains a separate public bar. The comfortable lounge has a cottage feel about it with part panelled walls and padded window seats. As recently as 1991 an old barn at the end of the building was converted into a large restaurant and family area. At the side, and front, are lots of picnic benches, and at the back a large children's play area.

Originally a freehouse, the pub is now owned by Hall & Woodhouse, very well managed by Nigel and Kathy Carr. There are two real ales; Badger Best and Tanglefoot Ale.

Food is available seven days a week with a Sunday roast. You can choose from the set menu or pick one of the daily specials chalked on the blackboard. There are pub snacks such as Ploughman's and salads plus a steak and salad French stick. Each day there is a home-made curry. Other popular dishes include a selection of tasty home-made pies. There are various steaks including 'steak Orlando' with stilton cheese, gammon, a mixed grill and good old English fish and chips. Children have their own menu.

Week day opening times are from 11 a.m. till 2.30 p.m. and from 6.30 p.m. till 11 p.m.

Telephone: (0929) 552909.

On the A3075 Wareham to Blandford Road, two miles north of Wareham.

Approx. distance of walk: 3¾ miles. O.S. Map 195 SY 903/898.

The inn has its own car park but it is just possible to park a car, back from the verge, in the road at the front.

An enjoyable walk through Wareham Forest and across cold Harbour Heath. It is easy going on large wide established tracks and well marked paths, making it ideal for all members of the family. Whilst mostly dry underfoot there are a couple of sections than can be a bit muddy.

The first half of the walk takes you through a pine forest. As the land is privately owned by the Morden Estates Company, and only let to The Forestry Commision, it is kindly requested that you keep to the marked paths. Bear left from the pub, cross the road and go into the woods. Follow the marked drive to the left. It skirts close to the edge of the wood before joining with a larger track from the right. Keep straight ahead, past farm land on the left, until you reach a wide forestry track on the left, one side of which has recently been planted with young fir trees. Turn left here.

The track is fairly long; at one point it crosses a small bridge, after which it bears left. When you reach the crossing point of a smaller track, turn left making your way past the watch tower, and through the metal gate on to the bridlepath through the woods. It is signed and easy to follow. Cross the

bridge and continue along the path between woods and the caravan site, eventually meeting the road.

Walk straight across, turn left, then immediately right on to the bridlepath, it is signed. The path through the trees is easy to follow, blue arrows painted at intervals marking the way. At one point, when you reach a clearing, turn left making for the corner of the caravan site and then turn right, look for the blue arrow. Keep close to the wire fence on the left. The path is easy to follow, but does require a little care as the surface is very uneven in places.

Before reaching the overhead power cable you will, see a signed footpath on the left. Turn here walking until you reach the forest, then take the wide track on the left. after a while the path bears right, into the woods, and down to meet the road. Turn left back to the pub.

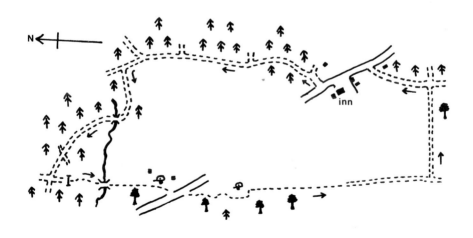

The sketch maps in this book are not necessarily to scale but have been drawn to show the maximum amount of detail.

The Castle Inn, Corfe Castle

This cosy 300 year old stone inn is very much a locals' pub with a pool table and dart board. From the street you walk directly into the main bar with its lovely flagstone floor, bare stone walls and heavily beamed ceiling. At one end is a lovely old open fireplace with seats around the wall. At the other end is a similar open fireplace with a warm wood burning stove. Just off the main bar is a small family room and dining area. A small front terrace has several picnic benches with more on the lawn at the rear.

The Castle is a Whitbread Inn with two of their real ales served from handpumps: Flowers Original and Whitbread Best Bitter.

A small but comprehensive food menu is available both lunch time and in the evening. There are the usual pub snacks such as soup, ploughman's, salads and jacket potatoes. You can also have breaded mushrooms with a dip or garlic bread. Main meals include cottage pie, steak and kidney pie and lasagne.

Children are allowed in the back room and dogs are welcome provided they are kept under control.

The inn is open at lunch time from 11 a.m. till 2.30 p.m. Monday to Wednesday, and 3 p.m. for the rest of the week. The pub opens in the evening at 6 p.m. and closes at 11 p.m.

Telephone: (0929) 480208.

Coming from Wareham, on the A351, the inn is on the left; the Swanage side of the village.

Approx. distance of walk: 3½ miles. O.S. Map No. 195 SY 963/817.

The inn has only a small car park. When busy it is better to park outside a few yards further down the road.

A most enjoyable scenic walk in The Purbeck Hills, ideal for a summers evening, not too demanding and fairly dry underfoot.

A small drive runs down beside the pub car park giving access to the playing fields at the back. Turn right and go across the field, through the gate in the far hedge and bear left down the field to the stile behind the stone building. Turn left and follow the path on the right up to a stile by the railway line. go through the cutting under the track, over the stile and turn right. Keep fairly close to the hedge on the left following the path up the meadow. If you are out walking early in the day you can very often find a number of delicious field mushrooms.

Continue through the gap in the hedge bearing left to the metal gate at the top. Head down the field and out through the gate to the left of the new house, into the field ahead, and down to the wooden crossing point in the far bottom corner. During very wet weather it is necessary to cross a small stream. The footpath continues up the fields, through a gap in the far hedge and then straight ahead to a gate. Go through and bear right, up to the top of the field, round to a stile and then across to the gate. Walk past the old stone barn and left, down across the field towards Tabbit's Hill Farm. Make your way up and round to the left of the buildings, out through the gate into the lane and turn left.

Go up to the T junction and turn left walking along the lane until you reach the bridleway on the right, signed to 'Branscome Hill ½'. Various plants can be seen growing along the track include Hartstongue fern, red campion and the 'stinking' iris *foetidissima* whose un-impressive flowers are more than compensated by the glorious red seed heads. At the top the track bears left offering you a choice of routes. The higher more scenic path takes you along the top of Rollington Hill, the lower, less exposed path is the more interesting and the one I prefer. It follows the hedgerow all the way back to the village. Blackberries and sloes grow in abundance and there are numerous clumps of prickly evergreen Butchers Broom.

Both paths meet again close to the village. Go up to the gate, out into the lane and turn left. Just past the cottage you will see the signed footpath on the right. Go into the field and round until you reach a gate on the right. Go through, cross the bridge over to the gate opposite, up the steps and over the railway line, back through the gate, across the playing field to the pub.

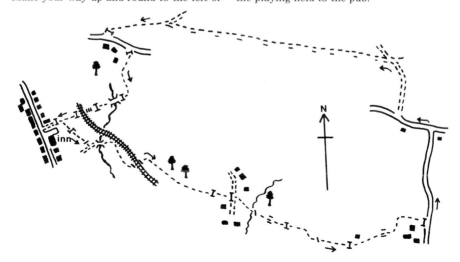

The Seven Stars, East Burton

The name Seven Stars is often given to a pub close to a bridge – it refers to the Patron Saint of Bridge Builders, St. John of Neponnick, whose sign this was. I am told the original pub at East Burton occupied a small stone building beside the present entrance. Today the pub sits in its own grounds high up in a sunny position close to the River Frome. The large modern exterior belies its recently re-fitted interior. The one long bar is divided into three sections. One end is an attractive restaurant area the other has bar games. The main bar has a heavy beamed ceiling and part panelled walls. Comfortable furnishings consist of old farmhouse tables, chairs and wooden settles. There is even an old bow legged Victorian dining table. Because of the obvious proximity to the river lots of fishing regalia adorn the walls. Outside are picnic benches both on the sunny terrace and the extensive lawns.

The inn is a Devenish house serving three real ales: Draught Bass, Marston's Pedigree and Royal Wessex.

Food is ordered from a separate bar between 12 noon and 2 p.m. and 6 p.m. till 9 p.m. in the evening. There are snacks such as ploughman's, and home-made soup. When I last visited the inn I had sea asparagus soup, quite unusual but delicious. A blackboard in the bar lists the daily specials. There are various steaks, gammon, omelettes and salads.

Children are allowed in the restaurant area although it is not always necessary to eat. Dogs are also welcome if kept under control.

Opening times are from 11 a.m. till 2.30 p.m. and again from 6 p.m. till 11 p.m. Telephone: (0929) 462292.

Village signed off the A352 at Wool and at Burton Cross.

Approx. Distance of walk: 5¾ miles. O.S. Map No. 194 SY 830/869.

Park at the front of the inn or on the grass parking area at the side.

A fairly long but very enjoyable country walk that twice crosses the River Frome, takes you to Bovington Tank Museum, through woods and into the small village of Moreton with its interesting church and graveyard where Lawrence of Arabia is buried. The going is easy making it an ideal walk for that family day out.

Leave the pub and turn left then left again at the crossroads. Follow the narrow lane round to the right and then left down to the river. Walk along the track and go over the small bridge, it is signed Bovington ¾. Bear left over the fields crossing as you do a series of bridges until you reach the edge of a small wood. Go over the stile and cross the bridge walking up through the trees then over the stile into the field at the top.

Keeping close to the hedge on the left, walk up the field following the little brook until you reach the stile which takes you out into the road. If you wish to visit the tank museum turn right and cross over to the entrance. Leave by the main entrance on the other side to pick up the walk again. Otherwise turn left and walk along the road. As you round the bend, almost opposite the main entrance to the museum, you will find a signed footpath running up alongside the army camp. Turn here, then cross Menin

Road when you reach the bottom and continue straight ahead following the track through the gate into the woods. Picnic benches have been provided should you wish to stop for some refreshment.

Keep to the main track through the woods and heath. When you eventually reach Snelling Farm the track bears right to meet a forest track from the right. Turn left over the bridge and fork right down to the river. Cross the bridge and continue ahead into Moreton. If you want to visit the village church of St. Nicholas go down the entrance on the left towards Moreton House.

Bear left at the road junction. The cemetery on the right is where T. E. Lawrence is buried. His grave is at the back on the right hand side. There is no other route back to the pub other than keeping to the lane. Although approximately only two miles it is an attractive walk, quite peaceful with very little traffic.

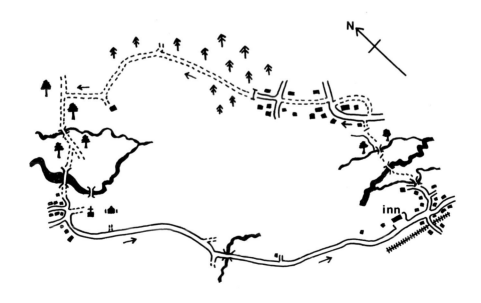

21

The Countryman, East Knighton

The Countryman Inn is a new pub but already has a delightful rustic atmosphere enhanced, I am sure, by the careful refurbishment of the existing cottages. From the front you enter directly into two cosy rooms each with a warm open fire but the main bar is at the back of the pub. There is a comfortable and attractive games room, a family room and a restaurant. Bare brick walls are much in evidence with lots of comfortable pine farmhouse chairs and tables. Outside there is a lawn beer garden and a kiddies play area. The inn is a family pub very well run by the owners Jeremy and Nina Evans.

A large well stocked bar offers a good range of drinks including four well kept real ales: Wadsworth's 6X, Courage Best, Directors Bitter, and my favourite, Ringwood's Old Thumper. The wine list has 22 bins plus house wine.

Very good home cooked food is served seven days a week till 2 p.m. at lunchtime and 10 p.m. in the evening. As all food is freshly prepared to order you may have to wait a while but you will be told how long by the courteous bar staff. A set menu and the carvery offers a good choice of meals to suit all tastes. There are the usual pub snacks such as ploughman's, filled rolls and sandwiches, also tasty home-made soup such as curried pea and apple. Fish dishes include butterfly prawns, pan fried sardines in garlic butter and 'salmon supreme' which consists of smoked and poached salmon combined with garlic mayonnaise. From the 'char grill' you can choose various steaks or how about the 'Countryman Grill' lamb cutlet, sausage, bacon, kidney, mushrooms, tomato, fried egg and saute potatoes. The blackboard in the bar offers tasty daily specials such as sweet and sour chicken, lasagne, chilli and steak and kidney pie. Vegetarians are well catered for. There is also a 'country kiddies corner' menu.

Accommodation is available, all rooms having en-suite bathrooms.

Weekday opening times are from 11 a.m. till 3 p.m. and from 6 p.m. till 11 p.m. Telephone: (0305) 852666.

The small hamlet of East Knighton is on the A352 about halfway between Wareham and Dorchester. The pub is a short distance down the gravel track which runs from the main road beside the garage. It is signed.

Approx. distance of walk: 3½ miles. O.S. Map No. 194 SY 811/857.

Park at the front of the pub, the lane at the side or in the large car park at the rear.

An easy walk, ideal for the whole family across heath and farmland which takes you around the perimeter of the Winfrith Atomic Energy Plant. In bad weather some of the paths can become a bit muddy, so adequate waterproof footwear is advisable.

From the inn turn left and continue down the stony track towards Winfrith Heath. At the point where the track bears left keep straight ahead following the path through the trees, bearing left when you reach the perimeter fence of the plant. The route could not be easier, simply follow the path close to the high fence walking all the way around. On the far side a grass track runs between the railway line and the fence leading to a tarred road.

Continue past the Police station to the main entrance of the plant and take the grass path on the left. Cross the bridge and turn left. Keep to the path ahead walking away from the perimeter fence, go through the small gate and round the field keeping close to the hedge on the left. Go through the gate on the far side then turn right across the small strip of field between the two hedges, left over the bridge and through the gate following the path ahead. It is all well signed.

After negotiating a couple of stiles a small bridge allows access to the field ahead. Bear left across to the gate, go through and turn left. Keeping close to the hedge, walk to the corner of the field, through the gate and turn right. Follow the path beside the hedge through two last gates, over the ditch and turn left to join a farm track which takes you straight back to the pub.

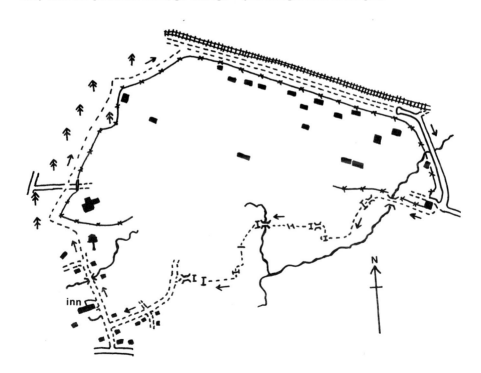

The Antelope, Hazelbury Bryan

If I had to make a preference on the sort of pub I prefer it would not be a modern pub nor would it have to be an old pub that had been modernised. It would be a traditional Dorset inn, one where I could feel relaxed, enjoy a pint of real ale and talk to genuine Dorset locals. A few such pubs still exist in Dorset and one of them is the Antelope at Hazelbury Bryan. This small rural village local still remains today much as it was at the turn of the century. An early photograph shows that it was once named The Commercial Inn. There is just the one main bar, simply furnished at one end with pub games at the other. There is a beer garden at the rear. The pub has been run by the same family since 1946. Miss Honeybun, the present licensee, took over from her father in 1987.

It is a Hall & Woodhouse pub happily still serving there Best Bitter in the time honoured tradition straight from the barrel.

Food consists simply of crisps, pies and freshly made, reasonably priced ploughman's lunches.

Children are restricted to the beer garden only.

Weekday opening hours are from 10.30 a.m. till 2.30 p.m. and from 6 p.m. till 11 p.m. Sunday the pub is open from 12 noon till 2.30 p.m.

Telephone: (0258) 817295.

This peaceful Dorset village can be easily reached from the A367 at Sturminster Newton.

Approx. distance of walk: 3½ miles. O.S. Map No. 194 ST 745/089.

Park at the front of the inn or in the road.

A lovely walk along peaceful country lanes, across farm land and through the small hamlets of Droop and Wonston. The going is fairly easy but can be wet in places during the winter.

Leave the pub and turn left, walking only as far as the lane on the right by the war memorial. It takes you down to Droop, a distance of just over a mile. The little church, dedicated to St. Mary & St. James, dates mainly from the 15th-century, although it does have a 12th-century font, a relic possibly from an earlier Norman structure.

On the right, beside the post box, is a farm gate. Go through it and straight across to a crossing point in front of a small clump of trees. Continue ahead, down the field, through a gate on the far side then make for the gate in the far left-hand corner. Go through, down the short grass track to the lane, and turn right.

Walk through Wonston turning left just past the telephone box. Follow the lane past several houses until you reach a signed footpath on the left. Go through the gate and walk down to the stile in the bottom corner of the field. Go over, and bear left, across to a pair of stiles in the far corner. Keep straight ahead over the little bridge, then across the field, through the farm gate

opposite, and turn right making for the gate to the left of the farm buildings. Go out into the lane and turn right.

As you round the bend you will see a farm gate on the left. Turn here and walk across the field to the gate in the hedge opposite. Go through into the field ahead and bear left, leaving by another gate in the far left corner. Bear right, walking round close to the stream, turning right when you reach the little stone bridge. The path of the bridleway runs across the meadow to the gate on the right of the house. Walk out onto the drive and turn right.

After only a short distance you will reach a grass track on the right, it is signed to Normead Drove. Turn here and keep walking until you see a small wooden gate on the left. Go into the field and, keeping close to the hedge on the left, make your way across to, and through the gap in the hedge by the large tree. Keep straight ahead, over the stile in the far hedge then continue in the same direction, out through the farm entrance into the lane, and turn right back to the pub.

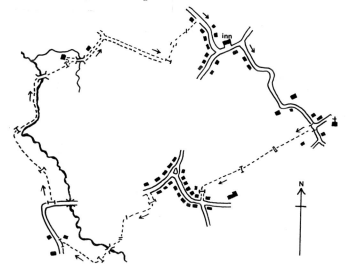

Cutt Mill

A Cottage Close to the Mill

The White Horse, Hinton St. Mary

Many strangers to the area travelling north on the B3092 from Sturminster Newton would have passed through the village of Hinton St. Mary probably unaware of the existence of this charming pub. This typical village inn is situated close to the church only a few yards from the main road. The public bar, with its quarry tile floor, is simply furnished with wooden wall settles and bar stools. At one end there is a small coal fire set into a large inglenook fireplace. The more comfortable lounge bar is also used as a dining room where families are welcome.

The inn is a freehouse well run by the owners. There are three real ales which usually include: Hook Norton Bitter, Wadsworth 6X and Ringwood Bitter.

Food is available seven days a week. On Sunday, when a roast is served in the dining area, snacks only are served in the public bar. The list includes ploughman's and sandwiches both plain and toasted. Jacket potatoes come with an interesting selection of fillings, curry of the day, bacon and mushroom, cheese, apple and nuts etc. There is also home-cooked ham and various omelettes. The main menu offers eight starters followed by various steaks, and home-made dishes such as steak and onion pie, curry with brown rice and rabbit pie. Chicken breast comes filled with prawns and lobster and turkey filled with asparagus and ham. There are five fish dishes and a separate menu for vegetarians which include Caribbean Medley served with salad and granary bread, a tasty lentil bake, also pasta and mushroom garlic sauce.

Children are permitted but only in the lounge. Dogs too if kept under control.

Weekly opening times are from 11.30 a.m. till 2.30 p.m. and from 6.30 p.m. in the evening till 11 p.m.

Telephone: (0258) 72723.

Walk No. 50

From Sturminster take the B3092 to Marnhull. when you reach the village turn right opposite the telephone kiosk. The pub is a short distance ahead opposite the lane to the church.

Approx. distance of walk: $3\frac{1}{4}$ miles. O.S. Map No. 183 ST 787/162.

The inn has its own car park at the back but it is quite safe to park in the surrounding lanes.

A most enjoyable walk from this delightful north Dorset village. The going is fairly easy but, as much of the walk is across farm land, it is best walked during fine weather. Cutt Mill, on the River Stour, is a lovely peaceful place; somewhere to stop during the walk to gather your thoughts. It is in fact the very spot that William Barnes chose to write several of his poems.

Leave the inn and turn left. Follow the lane round, and down through the village taking the second turning on the left. Ahead of you, at the end of the lane, is a stile beside a farm gate. Go over and follow the track down to the bottom, bear right and then left walking to the side of a narrow belt of trees. Further ahead the footpath bears left and then right on to a grass field before reaching a field.

Bearing slightly right, walk across to the hedge on the far side. Cross in the same direction making for the far right-hand corner. Again cross a bridge and wooden fence and, keeping close to the hedge on the right, walk to the far side of the field, out through the gate into the lane and turn left.

When you reach the road junction turn left and then right on to the Stalbridge road. After several yards you come to a farm on the left. Turn here, and keeping close to the hedge on the left, follow the track into the field. At the bottom is a stile. Cross over and turn left following the narrow path beside the pond, through the small copse, over the stile and into the field. Walk straight across to a pair of stiles in the far hedge. Go into the field ahead and turn right, through the gap in the corner then bear left, down across the field to the stile close to the river. Turn left following the river bank, over another stile, to the mill.

Go up the lane and as you round the bend look for a gap in the hedge on the right, it leads through to a small wooden gate. Go up into the field and bear right keeping close to the hedge. Continue ahead though another gate and onto a farm track. Turn right and then left following the path beside the woods, out on to the gravel track at the far side, and turn left back to the village and the pub.

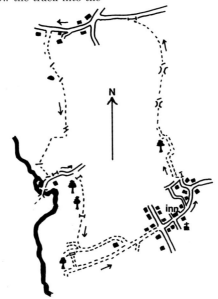

The Scott Arms, Kingston

Once an old coaching inn this attractive stone built pub is part of the Encombe Estate and occupies a unique high position with glorious views towards Corfe Castle. It was originally The Eldon Arms till Col. H. E. Scott bought the estate in the last century. The original building has been added to over the years and more recently an old barn at the back was converted into an attractive bar and restaurant area. From the small front stone porch the main bar leads off to the right. It has bare stone walls, wood parquet flooring and a lovely warm log fire in an attractive fireplace. Seating is provided by a number of old chairs and settles around an assortment of old tables. Across the other side of the hallway is the family room which has just been extended. It too has bare stone walls, a wooden floor and a very large open fireplace with a padded seat guard. Around the wall are comfortable settles and window seats together with other chairs and tables. From the lovely beer garden at the back you have what must be one of the best views in Dorset.

The inn is a Devenish house very well run by the new tenants. Three well kept real ales are served by hand pump: Wadsworth 6X, Flowers Original Strong Ale and Royal Wessex Bitter.

The food menu is chalked on the blackboard at the back of the new servery. Snacks include home-made soup, ploughman's, smoked salmon pate, breaded mushrooms and filled jacket potatoes. Followed by main meals such as 'Poulet a' Deux' which is chicken and peppers cooked in a creamy white wine sauce and Fisherman's pie – fresh fish and shellfish in a creamy sauce topped with potato and cheese. There is also home-made shepherd's pie, steak and kidney pudding, Dorset ham and turkey. The sweet list includes bread and butter pudding and Dorset apple cake.

Weekday opening times are from 11 a.m. till 2.30 p.m. and 6 p.m. till 11 p.m. Telephone: (0929) 480270.

Walk No. 51

On the B3069 two miles south from Corfe Castle.

Approx. distance of walk: 3¼ miles O.S. Map No. 195 SY 956/797.

There is plenty of parking in the pub's own small car park at the front and the larger one at the rear. You can also park safely in the road or in the car park just beyond the church.

Kingston is one of several small Purbeck villages in this delightful part of Dorset. This popular scenic walk down to Chapman's Pool has long been a favourite of mine, and although not a long walk, it is not all easy going. The path and steps down Houns-Tout cliff are quite steep and can be very slippery when wet.

From the pub turn right, walk up the lane past the church, turning left into the private drive to Encombe House. After a while the drive bears down to the right. At this point take the track on the left, it is signed to 'Houns-Tout'. Keep straight ahead over the stile beside the gate and follow the ridge. You get a good view in the valley of Encombe House.

Continue through three more gates and stiles. As you reach the head a seat is provided to enjoy the view west towards Kim-meridge. Go over the stile and continue ahead down Houns-Tout steps. Proceed with care as the path runs very close to the cliff edge, also the steps are very steep and can be slippery.

At the bottom go over the stile on the left and straight across the field heading inland following the stone wall up to the stile on the right. Go over and follow the path across to the tarred track then turn left. Keep straight ahead, over a couple more stiles, past the church back to the village.

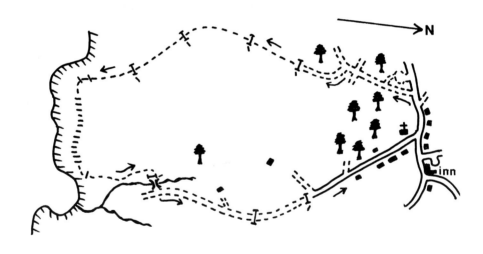

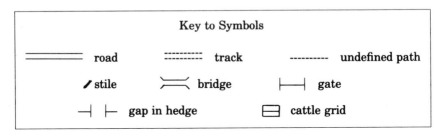

Key to Symbols

road .... track ---------- undefined path

/ stile ⟩⟨ bridge ⊢—⊣ gate

⊣ ⊢ gap in hedge ▭ cattle grid

Fox & Hounds, Little Canford

The attractive thatched Fox & Hounds is in a lovely spot, close to the River Stour, and surrounded by fields. Today it is very much a commercial family pub, but I remember a time, not many years ago, when there was just two small cosy bars and a charming bar billiard's room. The public bar is now a very good dining area while the original low beamed bar has been extended to accommodate a family room. There are lots of comfortable chairs, wooden settles and a chesterfield settee by the large inglenook fireplace. The bar billiard table survived but the room was knocked into the dining area; the bar itself is now accommodated in an extension at the back, the only part of the pub where children are not permitted. Outside there is a large lawn, beer garden and children's play area. In one of the adjoining fields there are some farm animals.

The inn is a Whitbread house presently offering three real ales on hand pump: Whitbread's Bitter, Flower's Original and Boddington's Bitter.

Considering the large number of meals served each day the food is very good. It is ordered from a separate servery where the daily roast is displayed in a glass fronted cabinet. A blackboard offers daily specials such as sweet and sour pork, meat and vegetable pie, large filled yorkies and 'fox pots' chilli and steak and kidney etc. From the set menu there are snacks of freshly made sandwiches, filled jacket potatoes, soup, cauliflower cheese and crispy mushrooms. Main meals include the landlord's grill, roast chicken, gammon, home-made lasagne and steak and kidney pie.

Opening times can vary but for most of the time and bank holidays the pub is open all day from 11 a.m. till 11 p.m.

Telephone: (0202) 872881.

Walk No. 52

The inn is set back from the road in a lane off the B3073 just south of its junction with the A31 at Canford Bottom.

Approx. distance of walk: 6¾ miles. O.S. Map. No 195 SZ 045/000.

There is a large car parking area at the pub, but it is quite safe to park in the lane at the front.

A very enjoyable walk around the Stour Valley. Apart from two very short sections along the highway the walk is entirely on bridleways and farm land. It is easy going and suitable for all members of the family but can become muddy during the winter.

Leave the inn and turn left along the lane, turning right at Little Manor Farm. Just before the road bridge go over the stile into the field on the left. Keep to the track around the field passing beside the small wood then go over the stile next to the gate. Bear left, through a second gate making your way across towards the river. Simply follow the path along the river bank crossing three stiles. The path then diverts from

the river, over a stile and gravel drive before a gate allows access back into the field. Head back towards the river where a bridge enables you to reach the far bank.

Turn left and then right when you reach the entrance to Canford School. Walk up through the car park, on to the pavement and continue ahead up through Canford Magna. After passing the last house on the left, go through the large white gates into

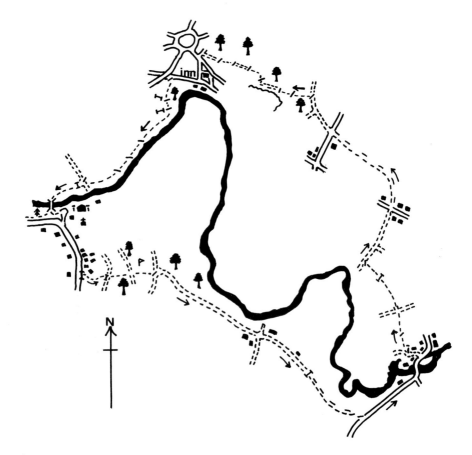

the field, the gate post is waymarked with a yellow arrow. Walk round the field, keeping close to the hedge on the left, go through the gate and straight ahead across the school playing fields. Once you reach the woods bear right over the ditch and walk to the corner of the field where you will find a path through the woods. It emerges on to a golf course. Simply walk straight across, obviously taking care to avoid any stray golf balls, following the route conveniently waymarked with yellow tipped posts.

A stile on the far side allows access to a gravel track. Continue straight ahead then follow the track to the right, passing through Knighton up to a farm gate. Go through and continue ahead across the field on the ancient drove road until a gate on the far side allows you to join the busy Ringwood road. Cross over and turn left. Walk over Longham Bridge then back across the road. On the left you will see a signed footpath to Hampreston Church. Turn here following the gravel drive until you reach a stile set in the hedge on the right. Bear left across the field, over to the wooden crossing point opposite and con-

tinue ahead. The path is well walked and easy to follow across the fields.

A stile ultimately brings you on to a gravel track. Turn right walking up to Ham Lane, go across the road and take the little path opposite, through a small wood and into the field. Continue ahead, keeping close to the hedge on the right. The path is well defined and eventually meets with Stapehill road. When it does walk straight across and down the gravel track opposite turning right at the fork. Further ahead you will see a stile on the left. Go over into the field and walk round, keeping close to the hedge on the left, crossing a stile in the wire fence. Continue to the corner of the field where a stile allows you to join a small path beside a stream running through the woods. After a short distance a stile gives access to the adjoining field. The path then bears left, and runs close to the hedge, crossing a couple more stiles, before entering into an area of tightly packed rhododendron bushes. The path emerges into a field. Continue ahead crossing a ditch and a stile, onto a narrow woodland path which finally brings you out in the road opposite the pub.

The Footbridge Across the Stour

33

The Rose & Crown, Longburton

The village of Longburton, together with nearby West Hall, was once owned by the Bishop of Salisbury. A map of 1564 clearly shows dwellings near the church. It is possible that the Rose & Crown was once the mason's church house. Later on it became a coach house and at one time brewed beer for the village with water from the well in the back room. The people of Longburton were always Royalists. In 1645 it is said a skirmish took place between Parliamentarians. It seems some soldiers took refuge in a room above the bar. During re-thatching, in 1946, a cavalier's sword (now in West Hall) was found in the roof. Presumably to keep in favour with both groups the then inn keeper had one side of the inn sign depicting a red rose and the other side a white one. Three comfortably furnished interconnected rooms are served by one central bar. There is a large inglenook fireplace at each end, one with a warm log fire. The inn has a skittle alley and there is an attractive courtyard at the back.

Although a tied pub for many years it is now a freehouse very well run by the proprietors, James and Josephine Smith. There are usually three real ales: Eldridge Pope's Dorchester Bitter, Thomas Hardy Country Bitter, Old Timer plus a guest beer such as Ringwood's Old Thumper.

The pub is well known locally for its good home-cooked food especially the Sunday roast. Apart from the usual snacks of tasty home-made soup and freshly made sandwiches you can have prawns served with a tangy seafood sauce, baked brie covered with mixed nuts, and mushrooms 'Rose & Crown style' – button mushrooms and strips of bacon served in a tarragon, garlic, wine and cream sauce. There is also a roast rack of lamb, poached salmon, various steaks and pan-fried whole plaice. Their own steak and kidney pie is very popular. Children are welcome, and dogs if kept under control.

Normal opening hours, which can vary with the seasons, are from 11 a.m till 2.30 p.m. and 6 p.m. till 11 p.m.

Telephone: (096321) 202.

The village is on the A352 Dorchester to Sherborne road 3 miles south of Sherborne.

Approx. distance of walk: 5 miles. O.S. Map No. 194 ST 648/128.

You can park in the pub's own car park or at the side by the church.

A very enjoyable walk a large part of which is on farm land. The walk takes you through Leweston Wood and the small hamlet at Folk. The going is fairly easy but can become muddy in wet weather.

Cross the road from the pub and walk up the short track to the stile beside the gate. Continue along the grass track, through another gate and into the field, it can sometimes be a bit muddy. Make your way over to the stile and, keeping close to the hedge, walk straight across the field to the stile in the far hedge, go down the steps, across the lane and follow the path into the wood opposite.

Take the right fork, over the pair of stiles into the field and bear left down to the kissing gate in the corner by the trees. Go out into the lane and turn left, walk over the bridge and up the drive towards St. Antony's-Leweston School. Just before the chapel turn left and walk across the lawn to the far fence, then bear right walking beside it until you reach the stile.

Go into the field and bear right across to the stile and follow the short path through the wood and out into the field ahead. Walk down to the bottom bearing slightly left, through the gap into the field ahead and over to the bridge. Cross into the field and continue in the same direction, out through the farm gate into the lane and turn left. Cross the bridge and go over the stile into the field on the right, it is signed. Bear left up to the gate in the top corner, go out into Bradford Lane and turn right.

When you reach the main village road you have two options, unless you only intend doing a short walk in which case turn left back to the pub. The most direct route is to cross the road and follow the bridleway ahead signed to Broke ½ but it is not advisable in very wet weather as part of the bridleway merges with a stream and can be 2 to 3 inches deep. The alternative is to turn right and walk down the road as far as a small chapel and then turn left up the gravel drive and immediately go over the stile into the field on the left. The path crosses to a

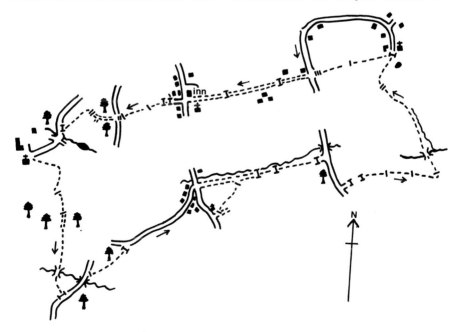

35

stile in the far left corner. Both paths meet at this point. Ignore the bridge across the river but turn right and follow the bank, through a small gate into a field, across to a similar gate and finally through one last gate out into the lane at Wizard Bridge and turn right.

After a couple of hundred yards you will see a signed bridleway on the left. Turn here and go through the gate, along the track, out through the gate and straight ahead, keeping close to the hedge on the left. Continue through another gate, across the field, through one more gate until you reach a pair of stiles in the hedge on the left. Go into the field and bear left down through the

gap in the opposite hedge and make your way along the bank to the bridge. Cross over and turn left following the course of the spring. When you reach the hedge turn left, go over the stile and make your way up the field towards the church of St. Lawrence.

There are two route options back. You can either walk through the village, round a couple of bends until you reach the farm turning, or cut across the field through a gate and down the steps to meet the lane. Which ever route you choose take the tarred drive through to West Hall Farm, it is signed, and continue ahead through a couple of gates until you reach the pub.

The Plough, Manston

Remotely situated just north from Manston this attractive stone pub was once an old farmhouse. The one beautifully kept bar was originally two rooms. There is a low beamed ceiling with attractive mouldings, a wooden parquet floor, bare stone walls and an assortment of chairs, tables and wooden wall settles. At one end is a stone fireplace. Outside there is a large beer garden overlooking the fields.

The inn is a feehouse run by the owner Mrs. Bidwell. There are usually two real ales: Badger Best and Ringwood Best.

Food is served seven days a week, all of it being home-made. There are the usual snacks of sandwiches and ploughman's, plus a choice of six starters including home-made soup and garlic mushrooms. Also omelettes, home-cooked ham, gammon and various steaks. Each day specials are chalked on the blackboard. Dishes such as roast lamb and salmon pasta in tarragon sauce with salad, and a dish for vegetarians, Bulgar wheat, cheese and vegetable bake with salad.

Children are not permitted in the bar, neither are dogs.

Weekday opening times are from 11a.m. till 2.30 p.m. and 6.30 p.m. till 11 p.m. Telephone: (0258) 472484.

01258 472484

The inn is situated on a bend in the road just north from Manston on the B3091 Sturminster Newton to Shaftesbury road.

Approx. distance of walk: 3½ miles. O.S. Map No. 183 ST 813/162.

Parking is limited to the pub's own car park.

A peaceful country walk, flat and easy going, mostly across farm land and through the small hamlet of West Orchard. As with many walks in this part of Dorset it can be very muddy. Try to walk during fine weather.

From the pub walk across the road into the driveway of Manor Farm and immediately go over the stile into the field on the right. Keep straight ahead to the far hedge where you will find two wooden crossing points and a small bridge. Continue ahead across to the metal gate in the hedge opposite, go through, and bear right round the field towards the farm. Cross the track, and go through the metal gate on the left, into the field and bear right making for the small gate in the top hedge. Go through and bear right, through the gate in the hedge and continue in the same direction over to the stile in the far corner. After crossing a narrow field a stile brings you out into the lane.

Turn left. A short distance ahead take the track on the right to Breach Farm. Just before reaching the entrance to the farm look for a crossing point in the hedge on the right. Go into the field, and keeping close to the hedge on the left, walk round past the pond and go immediately left through the hedge into the adjoining field. Bear right and walk diagonally across to the far corner where you will find a short track into the next field. Continue in the same direction making for the gate in the corner. Go

through and head towards the left-hand side of the farm buildings, out through the metal gate into the lane and turn right.

Take the turning on the left signed to West Orchard. Turn left at the road junction. Just past the church, on the same side of the road, you will see a short grass track on the bend. Go up to the farm gate, into the field and, bearing slightly left, walk across to the small gate in the hedge opposite. Go through, and keeping close to the hedge on the left, continue to the end of the field and through the farm gate. Immediately go over the stile on your left, then across the ditch and the stile into the adjoining field and continue ahead, this time close to the hedge on the right. A gate at the end of the field leads through to a track which takes you up to the road.

Turn right then left at the road junction on the Sturminster Newton road. After passing the third house on the right go up the signed footpath into the field and walk across making for the left-hand top corner, then go down to the gate in the far hedge. Bear right across to the corner of the field and exit through the gate in the hedge, across the grass strip and out through the entrance of Manor Farm to the pub.

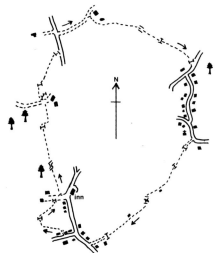

Blackmore Vale Inn, Marnhull

Throughout Dorset there are many old pubs that are steeped in history, many have connections with Thomas Hardy. The Blackmore Vale Inn is one such pub. It is referred to in his book, Tess of the D'Ubervilles as 'Rollivers'. Built some 400 years ago as farm cottages, and later becoming an old bake house and brew house, the cottages where eventually knocked through into the present delightful pub. There are two main bars both equally attractive having beamed ceilings, bare stone walls and two lovely old inglenook fireplaces with log fires in the winter. The inn has a skittle alley, a large beer garden and children's play area at the side.

Owned by Hall & Woodhouse it is very well run by the friendly licensees. Two real ales are available: Badger Best and the pale Tanglefoot.

A very good and imaginative food menu brings people from all around the area to dine. Available seven days a week, every taste is catered for. There are the usual snacks of filled jacket potatoes, sandwiches, ploughman's and home-made soup. From the main menu you can choose guinea fowl with Portland cranberry sauce or 'Hawaian Chicken' – breast filled with cream cheese, pineapple and ham. There are several steaks and grills including a 26oz T-bone, and a popular range of home-made pies. Fresh fish features very strongly on the menu. There is 'Dorset Tipsy Crab Pie' made with cream, whisky, cheddar cheese, lemon juice and parmesan cheese, salmon-en-croute, trout with a celery and walnut filling, lemon sole and usually something a bit different like red snapper or marlin.

Vegetarians can choose from at least six dishes such as chestnut patties in red wine and spinach and mushroom lasagne. Puddings include spotted dick.

Families are welcome in one of the bars and there is no objection to well controlled dogs.

Weekday opening hours are from 11.30 a.m. till 2.30 p.m. and 6.30 p.m. till 11 p.m. The landlord is considering the possibility of opening one or two afternoons for tea.

Telephone: (0258) 820701.

39

Walk No. 55

Marnhull can be reached from the north on the A30 and from the west on the A357 Blandford to Stalbridge road or more directly from Sturminster Newton on the B3092. The pub is on the Fifehead Magdalen road.

Approx. distance of walk: 3¼ miles. O.S. Map No. 183 ST 773/195.

There is a large car park behind the inn but you can also park safely in the road at the front.

An easy, mostly level walk across farm land which twice crosses the River Stour. Because of the obvious mud associated with the farms it is a walk for the summer.

From the inn turn right and then bear left walking to the end of Ham Lane. Go through the gate into the field and down to the bottom, keeping close to the hedge on the left. Go through the gate into the adjoining field and turn right, through another gate and cross the river. Keep straight ahead over to a pair of stiles and then bear left across the field towards Hamwood Farm.

On the right is a gate, it is waymarked. Go through and bear left, through another gate, into the farmyard and straight across, through the gate into the field opposite. Head over to the stiles in the hedge and then bear right. Just before reaching Crib House Farm you will see a pair of stiles in the hedge. Cross into the field and bear left, through the farm gate beside the barn, out on to the farm track and turn left.

As you round the bend to the farmhouse, go through the gate into the field on the right, it is signed. Bearing right, follow the waymarks, over a pair of stiles in the opposite hedge and make for the right-hand side of Gomershay Farm. Walk round be-hind the buildings, through a couple of gates, on to the farm track and turn left. Follow the track past the farmhouse then go left, over the stream, into the meadow and bear right across to the bridge.

When you reach the river, cross to the far side and make your way up to the farm gate. It is usually locked but there is a gap to climb through. Continue ahead, over the crossing point beside the gate, and up the lane ahead, past the cottages, turning left at the T-junction.

As you round the bend you will see a short drive on the left. Walk down to the farm gate, go through, across to a similar gate and then down the field to a stile. Continue ahead keeping close to the hedge on the right. On the far side of the field bear left past a small concrete structure, cross over the stiles and continue along the grass strip, through the farm gate and over the stile in the fence ahead of you. Follow the signed path to the left, up the track to the road, turning left back to the inn.

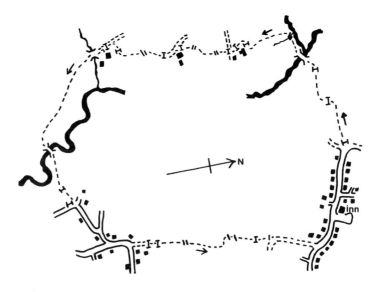

The Bottle Inn, Marshwood

The attractive, thatched Bottle is one of Dorset's traditional inns. It occupies a high position close to the Devon border overlooking the glorious Marshwood Vale. Dating back to 1585 it derives its name from the fact that it was the first pub in the area to sell bottled beer. Two cosy rooms are served by the same central bar. Both have white painted walls with heavy beamed ceilings. There is a small fireplace in one room and an attractive inglenook fireplace in the other. It is simply but comfortably furnished with chairs, tables and wooden wall settles, outside there is a beer garden and a skittle alley.

The Bottle is a freehouse well run by the owner Francis and her daughter, both qualified chefs. Two real ales are delivered by handpump: Exmoor Ale and Wadsworth 6X.

Food is served seven days a week which includes a Sunday roast. The menu offers a choice of bar snacks or full a la carte. Meals are all home-made and freshly prepared on the premises. Snacks include soup, sandwiches, various ploughman's, salads and home-cooked ham. From the main menu there is a choice of five starters and an interesting selection of main course meals such as scampi provencal, veal holstein, beef olives plus various steaks. Vegetarians have a choice of three dishes. Each day there are a few blackboard specials such as rabbit pie or a fish pasty.

Children are welcome and have their own menu. There is no objection to dogs.

Opening times during the week are from 11 a.m. till 2.30 p.m. and from 6 p.m. till 11 p.m.

Telephone: (029 77) 254.

41

Walk No. 56

The inn is situated close to the Devon border on the B3165, high up overlooking the Marshwood Vale.

Approx. distance of walk: 4½ miles O.S. Map No. 193 SY 378/997.

The inn has a small car park at the front.

A fairly difficult but very enjoyable scenic walk. The going is quite hilly in places and can be wet and muddy. When I last walked the paths in 1990 there were very few waymarks and not many stiles. At times you may find it necessary to climb barbed fences and walk through an occasional stream.

Walk straight across the road from the pub and go through the gate by the post box. Walk down and across to the gate in the far hedge, go through and continue ahead, keeping close to the hedge on the right, through a couple more gates and out through one last gate on to a track.

Turn immediately left and go through the gate on the left following the grass track until a gate eventually brings you into a field. Walk across, bearing left, to the far bottom corner. Go up through the gate and straight ahead, through the gap in the hedge than across towards the farmhouse. Climb over the fence and walk up the drive opposite, signed to Higher Spinhay.

Bear left through the gate beside the farm buildings and walk to the bottom of the field, go over the crossing point, out onto the track and turn left. Walk straight through the farm, through the gate and up the field, bearing slightly left. When you

reach the hedge look for a crossing point close to the large oak. Continue down to the bottom of the field, through the gap in the hedge, cross the stream and head up the field in the direction of Bettiscombe. You leave the field by a gate at the top.

St. Stephen's church dates from around the 14th-century. An interesting booklet on the history of Bettiscombe can be bought in the church. Turn left walking along the lane for about a third of a mile. As the road dips down you will reach a gate on the left opposite a grass track. Go through this gate and bear left across the field, through the gap in the hedge and down to the gate at the bottom. You can clearly see the route to be taken up the field opposite. Go through a gap in the hedge, up through a gate and then bear slightly left, out through the gate at the top, into the road and turn left.

From here you can walk straight back to the pub but there is a footpath you can use

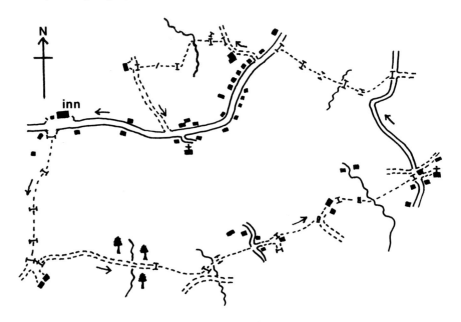

42

for about half of the distance; unfortunately it does mean crossing a stream and wire fencing.

When you reach a short track on the right to Tanyard Farm, go up to the farmhouse, through the farm gates, and then through the gate into the field on the left. Continue across to the far gate, into the field ahead and make your way to the stream at the bottom corner of the field. There is no bridge so get through as best you can, climb up the bank, over the wire fence, and bear left up the field. Go through into the field ahead making for the hedge on the right, turning right when you reach the gate. Keep close to the hedge on the left. A stile further ahead allows easy access into the next field. Make for the gate by the farmhouse, go through and turn left up the drive to the road. Turn right back to the pub.

The author relaxing having completed one of his walks from his first "Pub Walks in Dorset". *Photo courtesy of Southern Newspaper PLC.*

The Cock and Bottle, Morden

Happily there still remains in Dorset a number of lovely unspoilt rural pubs. The Cock & Bottle at Morden is one of them. Situated in a peaceful village setting yet only minutes from the busy towns of Poole and Wareham. The warm welcome from Pete and Gill, whose enthusiasm and obvious dedication as publicans, together with the charm and character of the pub all make for a great atmosphere; one that I would certainly want to come and experience again. The simply furnished main 'Chatters bar' has a tiled floor and a large open fireplace at one end, beside which is a large curved wooden settle; a cosy spot on a cold winters evening to warm yourself in front of the crackling log fire. The other carpeted bar has a comfortable restaurant feel about it with farmhouse chairs, tables and cushioned wall settles. A separate room off the lounge doubles as a family room and additional dining space.

The inn is owned by Hall & Woodhouse serving three real ales: the delightful pale Tanglefoot and their Badger Best, also Eagle Bitter from the independent Bedford brewer, Charles Wells.

Good home-cooked food is available seven days a week. Apart from snacks such as ploughman's and toasted sandwiches you can have home-made chilli, thick cut ham, chicken kiev, home-made beef in beer casserole and various steaks. And for vegetarians, a broccoli quiche. A specials board in the bar usually has one or two dishes such as home-made chicken curry or steak and kidney pie. Various home-made sweets include Dorset apple cake and apple pie.

A separate menu for children is available. Dogs are welcome provided they are kept under control.

Opening times are from 11 a.m. till 2.30 p.m., 3 p.m. at weekends and 7 p.m. in the evening until 11 p.m.

Telephone (092 945) 238.

Morden is a peaceful, unspoilt village lying on the B3075, 5 miles north of Wareham.

Approx. distance of walk: 3½ miles. O.S. Map No. 195 SY 913/947.

There is a small car park to the side of the inn and a lay-by opposite some houses.

A most enjoyable walk in beautiful unspoilt countryside. It is mostly on established paths, bridleways and country lanes, across farm land and through woods. Whilst easy going the bridleways do become very muddy in wet weather.

Go up the lane, opposite the pub, towards East Morden. Before reaching the village there is a signed footpath on the right next to the farm gate. Follow the path up beside the woods, out into the lane and turn left. At the top of the lane, where the road bears left, continue ahead onto the bridleway, it is signed 'Dolmans Hill 1 mile'. Go only as far as the stile, then into the field and bear left. At the bottom, behind a row of large oaks, is a stile set in the fence. Go over and cross the bridge following the well signed path up through the woods, over the stile at the top and into the field.

Turn left and make your way across towards the large electricity pylon. Bear right, over to the stile and cross the field to the stile at the top. Turn left onto the bridleway, it is signed 'Goodwin's Lane ½'. Take care as you go it can become quite muddy and slippery. At the bottom a footpath joins with the bridleway. Go over the stile and through the woods until you reach a gravel track close to the pylon. To rejoin the path keep straight ahead into the woods opposite

and turn left. The path follows the perimeter of the woods before re-emerging on to the track. Walk straight across, through the narrow strip of woodland and over the bridge to rejoin the track. Walk down the hill to the bottom, go over the stile and up the field to another stile at the top. Turn left and follow the path down, through the edge of the wood, to meet the lane.

Bear right and walk down the lane turning left at the road junction towards East Morden. Just before reaching the church turn left down the 'no through' lane, past several houses, over the stream and up the short grass track to the gate. Go into the field and turn right. Walk round keeping close to the right-hand hedge. About half-way across you come to a stile either side of a small bridge. Go across into the field on the right and turn left. Keeping close to the hedge on the left, continuing ahead to the gate in the far corner of the field. Go out into the lane and turn left following the lane back to the pub.

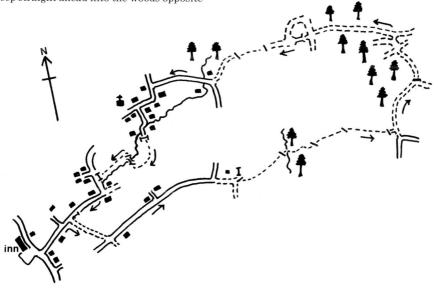

The Halfway Inn, Norden

Little is known about the history of this delightful old thatched pub apart from the fact it was originally a farmhouse built some 400 to 500 years ago and is a grade II listed building. It has probably changed little over the years although plans are in the air to refurbish the interior so as you read this report it could well be out of date. I hope they do not alter it too much and spoil the character. As you enter the age of the inn is immediately apparent having irregular boarded walls, leaning doorways and low beamed boarded ceilings. There are three rooms: a small cosy lounge, simply furnished with a warm coal fire, a public bar still with the original flag stone floor, and an L-shaped bar at the back.

It is a Whitbread House with one real ale Strong Country Bitter.

The friendly tenants, May and George, are building a reputation locally for their very good food. George is from Cyprus and this is reflected in the menu. His range of 'lite bites' include Greek dips of taramasalata and houmos, with which you can have mushrooms filled with stilton in a crispy batter, fried halloumis (Cypress cheese), whitebait, garlic mushrooms, etc. Also home-made soup, plough-man's, jacket potatoes, sandwiches, lasagne, home-cooked ham, moussaka, chilli and a choice of home-made curry. In addition there are usually several daily specials such as spicy donar kebabs, liver and onions and a home-made bake of courgettes in tomato and cheese. If you are still hungry there is mouth watering choice of sweets like treacle tart, steamed syrup pudding, apple crumble and pancakes filled with raspberries on a brandy flambé with cream.

Families are welcome but no dogs.

Weekday opening times are from 11 a.m. till 2.30 p.m. or 3 p.m. and 6 p.m. till 11.30 p.m.

Telephone: (0929) 480402.

The pub is on the A351 about halfway between Wareham and Corfe Castle, presumably how it got its name!

Approx. distance of walk: 3½ miles. O.S. Map No. 195 SY 937/843.

The pub has its own large car park. There are few other places where one can park safely.

A most enjoyable walk, easy to follow, ideal for the whole family which takes you through Furzebrook and Norden Wildlife Reserve. The reserve has areas of heath, wet grassland, lakes and woodland. The undulating scenery is particularly attractive, the result of past clay extraction. In late spring many of the paths are carpeted with primroses. I prefer to walk here in late spring or early summer all other times it can be extremely wet and boggy in places.

Leave the inn and turn left. Almost immediately you will see a signed footpath. Turn left here. The tree lined path dips down and passes through a rather wet area where the path crosses a small stream before rising up on to the heath. Bear right and follow the winding path, it is well marked with the occasional wooden post. Go under the railway bridge and turn right, over the stile, following the fenced path to the stile at the far end, then walk up to the road and turn left.

Furzebrook is a peaceful village especially in the winter but does get busy during the summer with visitors to the Blue Pool. Having passed the entrance to the Blue Pool, keep walking until you reach the point where the road bears right then cross over and follow the signed path ahead into the woods. On the far side go out through the gate and turn immediately left on to the bridle path.

After a while you will see a signed footpath on the left, No. 9. It is not necessary to take this path but it is worth the diversion as it skirts one of the lakes. Simply follow the signs round the lake which eventually bring you back to the bridleway. After passing a small pond the bridle path bears right but continue ahead on to footpath No. 11. In late spring the path is carpeted with primroses.

After winding your way through the trees you will eventually reach the junction of two other paths, cross over and bear left on to path no 12, signed to the Blue Pool. Again the route across the heath is well marked. When you reach the junction of path No. 13 turn right, that is of course unless you want to visit the Blue Pool, in which case turn left. The path crosses the railway line before reaching the road. Then turn left back to the pub. There is a wide grass verge on both sides of the road.

The Royal Oak, Okeford Fitzpaine

Okeford Fitzpaine has many listed buildings and is one of Dorset's most attractive villages, especially the view east looking towards the church. The Royal Oak is a typical village local. It is an old inn dating back to the 17th-century still, traditionally, with two bars. The simply furnished public bar has its original flag stone floor, oak panelled walls and a beamed and boarded ceiling. One wall is dominated by a lovely large open, brick built, inglenook fireplace with a warm log fire in winter. A small family room off to the side has a bar billiard table. The cosy carpeted lounge has an attractive fireplace, comfortable furnishings and wall settles. There is also a skittle alley and an attractive beer garden at the back.

The pub is a freehouse well run by the owners Brian and Jacky Hall. The real ale served is Badger Best Bitter.

Pub food is available every day but Wednesday, most of which is home-made. Various snacks include sandwiches, hot soup, farmhouse pate, ploughman's lunches, various jacket potatoes and salads. There are two pies, steak and kidney and fisherman's. Also ham off the bone, a medium beef curry, home-made chilli and lasagne, as well as sirloin steak and home-made quiche. Several sweets include home-made fruit crumble.

Children are welcome as long as they are well behaved and there is no objection to dogs.

Normal opening hours are from 11 a.m. till 2.30 p.m. and 6.30 p.m. until 11 p.m. Telephone: (0258) 860308.

Village best reached from Shillingstone off the A357, Blandford to Sturminster Newton road.

Approx. distance of walk: 4 miles. O.S. Map No. 194. ST 805/110.

The inn has its own car park at the back but you can park safely in the village street.

A lovely open country walk mostly across farm land. Before returning to the village the walk takes you through the tiny hamlet of Belchalwell. It is fairly easy going but can become muddy during bad weather.

Leave the inn and turn right. After passing Parknoll Lane look for a track on the right, it is just past a house called Sleeply Hollow. Walk up to the house and, keeping close to the hedge on the right, go across the lawn to the stile in the hedge. Go into the field and make your way over to the pair of stiles set in the hedge then bear right down to another stile. Cross over into the field and bear left to a metal farm gate in the hedge. Continue in the same direction, through a gate in the top right-hand hedge, over to a

similar gate, and finally straight ahead leaving the field by the small gate in the hedge opposite.

The track rises slightly before dipping down to meet the lane. On the left is a signed bridleway. Turn left here. When you reach the field go through the gate and bear left, down across to the stile. Follow the short path through the wood, and cross over the stile into the field ahead walking up to the gate at the top, go out into the lane and turn left.

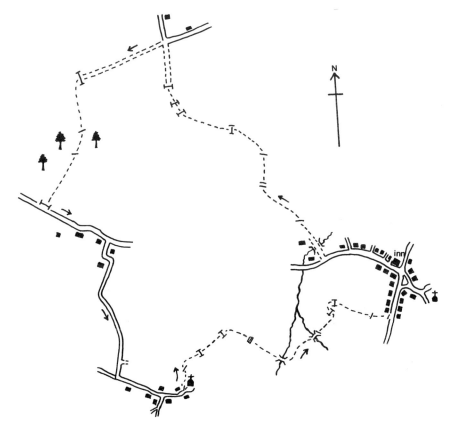

If you are feeling tired or want to cut short the walk the lane will take you straight back to the pub. To follow our walk turn right when you reach Garlands Lane. It is a fairly quiet and peaceful lane which eventually brings you into the small hamlet of Belchalwell.

Bear left up to the church, go over the stile on the left of the entrance gate, walk round the church and up to the crossing point in the left-hand corner of the field. Cross into the adjoining field and bear right down to the gate at the bottom, the path is signed. Try not to make the same mistake as I did and follow the vehicle track; instead bear left across the field to another farm gate in the opposite hedge, go through and then bear right over to a crossing point. Continue straight ahead down the field to the little bridge, cross into the field and bear left following the hedge round to another bridge and stile, then walk straight ahead across the field bearing left through a gate in the far hedge. Immediately turn right, through another gate and bear left across to a stile in the opposite hedge. Go over and down beside the hedge to the stile, out into the lane, and turn left back to the pub.

Okeford Fitzpaine

The sketch maps in this book are not necessarily to scale but have been drawn to show the maximum amount of detail.

St. Stephen's Church, Kingston Lacy, walk no. 60

St. Mary's Church, Chettle, walk no. 70

The Vine Inn, Pamphill

Throughout Dorset I know of few pubs that can compare with the delightful Vine Inn at Pamphill. It is set on a hillside, in a peaceful spot, close to the River Stour and surrounded by rolling green fields. The inn sign is one of the oldest in the country and refers to the Roman vineyards. It has not changed at all in the many years I have been coming here nor I suspect has it changed much for the locals who crowd into the tiny public bar. The small lounge bar is not much bigger it has seating for 12 at three small tables. Most people though enjoy sitting on the sunny front terrace. Some even play draughts, a game that has traditionally been played here for many years. The pub forms part of the Bankes Estate which is now the property of The National Trust.

The present tenants, Linda and Brian, hold the lease and run the pub as a freehouse. There is just the one real ale Whitbread's Strong Country Bitter.

Because of space restriction bar snacks are limited to freshly made ploughman's or sandwiches and then only served at lunch time.

Families are welcome so too are dogs.

Telephone: (0202) 882259.

About a mile out of Wimborne take the turning for Pamphill signed from the B3082, Wimborne to Blandford road. Turn left opposite the church. The pub is on the left, just beyond the school at the end of the drive.

Approx. distance of walk: 2½ miles. O.S. Map No. 195 ST/SY 995/003.

There is no car park as such but there are parking area's off the road close to the school.

To visit Pamphill is to step back in time. What was once part of the Bankes Estate is now the property of The National Trust. There are many walks around the Estate and places of interest to visit such as St. Stephen's Church, Kingston Lacy House and nearby Badbury Rings. The walk I have selected is ideal for all the family, it is fairly short and easy going along the banks of the River Stour.

Leave the pub and walk down to the bottom of Vine Hill, cross the road and go over the stile into the field. Before reaching the river, bear right, and follow the well worn path across to the stile and out on the track. Turn left and then go right, over the stile beside the gate, and follow the grass track. Do not cross the bridge. Eye Mead is an area of riverside meadows; an important grass area for animal feed. You can read the history of the area recorded on a plaque by the river.

The path is easy to follow needing little explanation. At one point a small bridge takes you over a tributary before rounding an enclosed field. Go through a gap in the wire fence and turn right, following the tree lined path. As you near the road cross over the bridge, and stile into the field, and bear right over another small bridge walking up to the road and turn right.

Turn left when you reach Holly Lane, it is opposite a large corrugated barn, the footpath is signed. Go up the track to the stile, across the yard and over the stile opposite. Follow the path to the stile at the top, go over, and cross the stile on the right, signed to Pamphill Green. Walk up the field, over another stile and keep straight ahead through the small gate on to the gravel track. At the top walk on to the green and turn right, past the thatched sports pavilion, out into the lane and turn right back to the pub.

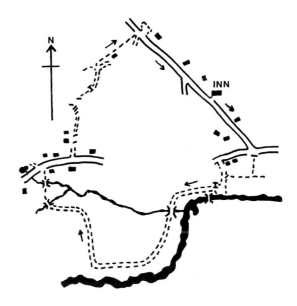

The European Inn, Piddletrenthide

The European Inn, so titled in the 1860's, is situated in the heart of Dorset in the beautiful Piddle Valley. How it got its name is not certain but it possibly recalls the numerous European wars this country was engaged in in the 18th to 19th-century. It is unique in the fact that it is believed to be the only pub with that name in Great Britain. Looking from the outside more like a private house the two storey inn occupies an enviable position overlooking the downs. Inside there are two interconnected rooms served by the one bar. A number of interesting artifacts are displayed around the walls and hung from the beamed ceiling. The furnishings are comfortable with cottage style chairs, tables and settles. There is an attractive open fireplace with a log fire in winter. Outside seating is provided on the lawn around the inn.

It is a freehouse beautifully kept and run by the present owners, Dave and Carol Pugh. For real ale lovers you can choose from Courage Best, and Piddle Ale, a beer brewed for the pub.

The menu offers a varied choice of English style cooking every day of the week. Apart from the usual snacks such as ploughman's, filled rolls and salads there is a choice of omelettes, home-cooked ham – carved off the bone and venison sausages. Various fish dishes include lemon sole stuffed with crab meat. There are steaks, grilled gammon and chicken kiev. Saute potatoes are offered as an alternative to chips. See the blackboard for the daily specials.

Opening times in the week are from 11 a.m. till 3 p.m. and 6 p.m. till 11 p.m.

Children are welcome but only when eating in the dining area. Dogs too if kept under control.

For anyone wanting to stay overnight there are three, comfortably furnished, double en-suite letting rooms.

Telephone: (03004) 308.

The inn is situated in the Piddle Valley on the B3143 about 5 miles north from Dorchester.

Approx. distance of walk: 4 miles. O.S. Map No. 194 SY 712/982.

The inn has its own car park at the back. You can also park safely in the lane at the side.

A scenic downland walk along farm tracks. It is easy going and mostly dry underfoot.

Leave the inn and turn right. Go down the lane at the side turning right again along the track behind the inn. Turn left at the junction and follow the lane up round past the houses and on to the bridle path. Keep going until you reach three gates, ahead of you and to the right. Go through the first one into the field on the right and follow the hedge round to meet another gate. Go through and straight across the field keeping to the track as it bears right, down through another gate, towards the farm buildings at the bottom.

Go through the farm gate and turn right. Continue up the concrete farm track, past the farm buildings and down towards the valley. As you round the second bend, just past a private dwelling, continue ahead through the farm gate and walk straight across the field to the gate on the far side. Go through, out onto the track and keep straight ahead. Ignore the track back to the road but keep walking until you reach the junction of four tracks then take the one on the left, through the hamlet, back to the pub.

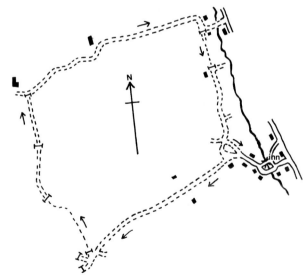

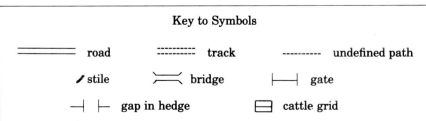

Key to Symbols

road ╱ track ----- undefined path

✔ stile ⟩—⟨ bridge ⊢—⊣ gate

⊣ ⊢ gap in hedge ⊟ cattle grid

The Anvil, Pimperne

Pimperne gets its name from the Celts who settled beside the river with 'five trees', thus named PIM-PREN. The Manor was later owned by Henry VIII and given to Catherine Howard for life. But we all know she soon lost her head after which Henry gave the village to Catherine Parr. The attractive, thatched Anvil Hotel dates back to 1535, and although added to over the years, much of that original building still survives. The main restaurant is a joy to behold. It has a heavily timbered ceiling, a lovely flagstone floor, and at one end, a large inglenook fireplace with a warm log fire. For a number of years the Anvil was just an hotel with a popular licensed restaurant but in 1990 became a full freehouse. The existing bar area has now become the lounge, both for residents and non-residents alike, and a new bar built blending well with the existing building. At the front is an attractive beer garden with much to interest children including a cage with a pair of rescued capucine monkeys.

There are two real ales on handpump; Flowers Original and Wadsworth 6X.

Food is served seven days a week; the bar menu being supplemented each day with a list of specials. The majority of the food is home-made including the bread rolls. There is always a tasty soup, sandwiches, salads and various ploughman's including crab in season. Also a fishbake – smoked flaked haddock in cheese sauce. Specials include snacks such as bubble and squeak, macaroni cheese, cottage pie and usually a vegetable bake. In the restaurant one can choose from a more comprehensive menu. There are fourteen starters alone. Main course meals include poached salmon and halibut or grilled dover sole plus various chicken dishes. 'Jacquinot' is poached breast stuffed with pate in a white wine sauce. There is pigeon, pheasant, various steaks and four tempting vegetarian dishes. Children have their own menu but are only allowed in the lounge and family room. Dogs are welcome provided they are under control.

The inn offers good accommodation approved by the Tourist Board.

Telephone: (0258) 453431.

The village is on the A354, just north from Blandford.

Approx. distance of walk: 4 miles. O.S. Map 195 ST 906/095.

The inn has its own car park at the front. Alternatively you can park safely in the lane at the side.

A very enjoyable and peaceful country walk, for the most part on wide, well marked bridle paths. The going is fairly easy making it ideal for all members of the family and novice walkers alike.

From the inn take the lane at the side walking towards the village centre. Turn right at the road junction and go up Down Lane towards the Post Office. Bear right at the top and continue along the track past the farm buildings on the left. The bridle path continues around the field but you can, if you prefer, short cut across the corner on footpath No. 3. If you decide to do that go through the farm gates into the field on the left and bear left, towards the woods in the distance. Half way across go through the farm gate in the fence and make for the right-hand corner of the wood to rejoin the bridle path beside the hedge.

Turn left and continue ahead through the farm gate and down to the bottom of the field. Cross the farm track and go up the large wide track ahead. After passing Pimperne Wood you reach a crossing track. Turn left here walking for a short distance before entering a field. Continue ahead, keeping close to the hedge on the left, into another field and round until you reach a stile in the corner of the field.

Cross over into the thicket. The path down to the bottom is not very clear but pick your way carefully keeping as close as possible to the field boundary on the left. When you reach the gate go through, on to the bridle path and turn left. The track continues ahead eventually merging with a tarred lane which leads back, past the church, through the village centre to the pub.

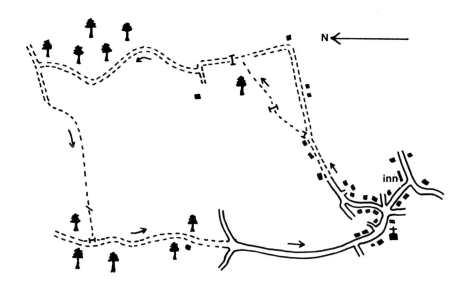

The sketch maps in this book are not necessarily to scale but have been drawn to show the maximum amount of detail.

The Kings Arms, Portesham

The area around Portesham has long been inhabited by man, evidence of such is still seen in the number of barrows scattered around the area dating from around 2500 BC. The earliest lies just north of the village on Ridge Hill. Nine massive stones, known as the Hellstones, are the remains of a long barrow built around 4000 BC. The Kings Arms was probably once the local of Captain Masterman Hardy who was born at Kingston and lived for a while in nearby Portesham House. The pub looks very much like a gentleman's residence, in fact the main bar was designed to look like his cabin on the Victory and at one time was known as 'Hardy's Bar'. The L-shaped bar has a games area at one end and a dining room the other. In the centre is a fireplace with a warm open log fire in the winter. Around the walls, and behind the bar, is an interesting collection of teapots. There is a large sunny beer garden and children's play area, an ideal place for families during the summer. A trout stream runs down beside the main village road a tributary of which passes under the road and through the garden of the pub.

The pub is owned by the Devenish Brewery and run by the licensees Brian and Julie Barrett. Real ale is traditionally served straight from barrels at the back of the bar. You can choose from Royal Wessex and the dry hopped Vallence's Bitter.

Food is available from the set menu with daily specials listed on the backboard. Pub snacks include soup, garlic bread, local ham, salads, traditional ploughman's and filled rolls. There is home-made steak and kidney pie, a hot chicken curry, chilli, lasagne and goujons of plaice. For pudding you can have home-made Old English pie made with raisins, sultanas, cinnamon, nutmeg and cloves.

Normal weekday opening times are from 11 a.m. till 2.30 p.m. and again from 7 p.m. (6 p.m. in the summer) till 11 p.m.

Children are only allowed in the dining area or garden. Dogs only in the garden. Telephone: (0305) 871342.

58

Nestling beneath the downs, west of Abbotsbury on the B3157, lies the lovely stone village of Portesham. If coming from the north on the A35 turn south at Winterbourne Abbas.

Approx. distance of walk: 3¼ miles. O.S. Map 194 SY 602/857.

Park either in the pub's own car park or in the village itself.

A very scenic walk which takes you across farm land and through woodland to the top of Black Down and Hardy's Monument. At seventy foot high, it is a stone column that was erected in 1844 as a memorial to Vice-Admiral Sir Thomas Masterman Hardy a trusted friend and shipmate of Nelson. The going is mostly dry underfoot but very hilly and demanding in places.

Leave the pub and turn right walking up through the village, past the shop turning right when you reach the bridle path on the right, signed to Hardy Monument 1½. Go up the track, through the gate, and bear right, up the field making for the track in the far top corner. Keeping close to the wall walk through the gate and down the field ahead until you reach a metal farm gate on the right. Walk through, out on to the stony track and turn left.

Go through the gate at the bottom and take the path on the left and then right up into the woods, signed 'Hardy Monument ½', keeping to the main path. Close to the top take the right fork, it is signed, 'to the monument'. At the top, after enjoying the view, leave the monument heading south east. A number of paths cross the heath, pick a suitable one and make your way down into the woods. When you reach a narrow track turn right following it down to join with the main track through the woods. At first it rises before descending to the bottom.

Go back through the farm gate and up the track keeping straight ahead. Walk past the farm, through the gate following the tarred track down to meet the lane. Go through the gate and turn right, turning left in the village back to the pub.

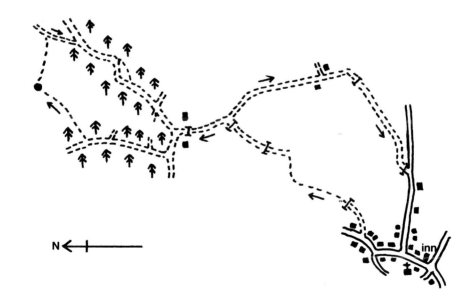

N ←—+———

The Crown Inn, Puncknowle

Puncknowle (pronounced Punnel) is a delightful village that existed well before the Roman occupation, evidence of Stone Age and Iron Age man can be seen all around. The delightful thatched Crown Inn is situated in the main village street opposite the 12th-century church and was once part of a row of cottages occupied by the monks. Today there are two bars with a family room at either end, both are comfortably furnished each with a warm open log fire in winter. The cosy lounge has bare stone walls, a large attractive fireplace, and extra seating provided by wooden wall settles and window seats. There is a beer garden at the back.

The inn is owned by Palmers, the local Bridport Brewery. In the well stocked bar are three real ales; Palmers Best, Bridport Bitter and the strong winter warmer Tally Ho.

Food is served seven days a week with a traditional roast on Sunday. A good range of snacks include something different – mushrooms in port served on toast. Other home-cooked dishes are beef and parsnip pie cooked in Tally Ho Bitter, game pie cooked in Guinness, fish pie in Palmers white wine, an unusual pie made with pork and water chestnuts cooked in Palmers ginger beer plus the good old favourite steak and kidney in stout. Vegetarians have at least five dishes of their choice and there is a children's menu. A selection of home-made sweets include treacle sponge and fruit filled pancakes.

Normal weekday opening times are from 11 a.m. till 2.30 p.m. and 7 p.m. till 11 p.m.

Dogs are allowed if kept under control.

Overnight accommodation is available and approved by the English Tourist Board.

Telephone: (0308) 897711.

The inn is best reached from the B3157 coast road between Abbotsbury and Bridport. If you are approaching from the north, on the A35, take the turning to Litton Cheyney.

Approx. distance of walk: 3½ miles. O.S. Map 194 SY 535/887.

Although the inn has its own car park at the rear it is quite safe to park in the road at the front.

A delightful walk in this lovely part of South Dorset. It is very scenic and not too demanding but there are a few hilly sections. Most of the walk is across open farm land which of course can be a bit muddy during bad weather.

From the inn turn left and left again into Looke Lane. As you round the bend on the lane junction go through the gate into the field, it is signed Litton Cheyney 1. Walk diagonally left to the far hedge, go through the gap and continue ahead across the field and down through the gap in the far corner. Keep walking in the same direction to the hedge on the far side. Go through the gap crossing the stream, the path is marked with a yellow arrow on a large stone. Continue in the same direction over the small stone bridge, then turn right, over the stile, crossing the River Bride, and over another stile into the field.

Bear left in the direction indicated by the yellow waymark towards Litton Cheyney village. Walk through the farm gate and up the field ahead until you reach a stile in the

6hedge. Cross the stream and stile, into the adjoining field turning left. Walk to the top of the field, left over another stile and finally out through the farm gate into the lane and turn left.

At the road junction continue ahead for a short distance towards the village. Almost opposite the White Horse, another Palmers inn, go over the stile into the field and bear right, up to and through the farm gate, into the field ahead leaving by the gate in the far hedge. Turn left and walk up the lane until it bears right. At this point keep straight ahead on the farm track, passing through the gate and following the track around Pins Knoll. On a clear day it is a glorious viewpoint.

Continue round the hill until the track descends towards the valley on the right,

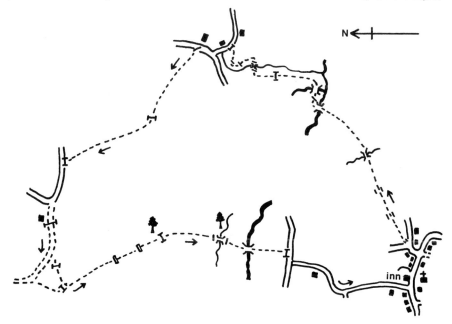

Walk No. 64

ahead of you is a gate leading into a field, a blue arrow on a post indicating the bridleway. Go through and down, keeping close to the hedge. When you reach a gate on the right, marked with the familiar yellow arrow, turn immediately left, and bear left, across and down the field to the far left-hand bottom corner. Go over the crossing point and down the field ahead, over another crossing making for the metal farm gate close to the corner of the wood on the left.

Walk to the bottom of the field where you will find a stile in the hedge, beyond which is a small bridge and a second stile allowing access to the field ahead. Continue over to the small stone bridge, once more crossing the River Bride, then up the field, out through the gate at the top, into the lane and turn right. A few steps further on turn left following the lane up to the village centre, turning left back to the pub.

The White Horse Hotel, Litton Cheyney

Key to Symbols

road   track   undefined path

✗ stile   bridge   gate

gap in hedge   cattle grid

The sketch maps in this book are not necessarily to scale but have been drawn to show the maximum amount of detail.

The Halsey Arms, Pulham

Deep in the heart of Dorset, on the edge of the Blackmore Vale, lies the small hamlet of Pulham with its pub The Halsey Arms. Landowning families, years ago, leased pubs on their estates to tenants and often insisted that their coat of arms be displayed to let everyone know who owned the property. The Halsey family married into the local landowning family of Henshaws and inherited the property through marriage. Dating back to the 17th-century, it was once an old coaching stop. Today it is owned by Joyce Westell and her family and is very much a local's pub with just the one main bar and a games room.

There is one real ale which could be Butcombe Bitter, Royal Oak or Hardy's Bitter.

A selection of pub snacks include sandwiches, plain and toasted, ploughman's, jacket potatoes, beef burgers and soup. Also lasagne, home-made chilli and the inn's own home-cooked ham with eggs. Children have their own menu. During the summer there are usually one or more daily specials.

Children are welcome in the pub and there is no objection to dogs.

Weekday opening hours are from 11 a.m. (12 o'clock in the winter) till 3 p.m. and 6 p.m. (7 p.m. in the winter) till 11 p.m.

Telephone: (0258) 817344.

Walk No. 65

Village on the B3143 about three miles south from the A3030.

Approx. distance of walk: 3½ miles. O.S. Map No. 194 ST 706/087.

The inn has its own car park but there is also a small parking area opposite the pub.

A very peaceful and enjoyable country walk mostly across farm land. It is best walked in dry weather, during late spring or early summer; it can become very muddy when wet.

Turn left from the inn and cross the road. After passing several houses turn right into the short drive leading up to the steel fabrication works. Ahead of you is a gate leading into a field. Go through, down to the gate at the bottom, and bearing slightly right, walk up the field ahead to the gate in the far hedge. Go through and make your way to the bottom right-hand corner of the field. Bear right over the stile, cross the bridge and turn left through the trees, crossing over the stile into the field.

Keep straight ahead, through the gap in the hedge opposite, then bear right making for a small gate in the corner of the field. On some occasions you may well see deer coming from the woods in front of you. Go through the gate and turn left. Keeping close to the woods on the left, continue ahead through a gate and down the field until you reach a farm track on the left. It takes you up to, and through, Harbins Farm into the lane. Cattle movements along the track can make it very muddy during the winter.

Turn right. After rounding the bend look for the stile on the left next to a gate. Go into the field and bearing right, make your way up to the far top corner, cross the stile and turn left. Keeping close to the hedge, walk round the field, past a small wood and through the gate into the field ahead. A few steps further on go through the gate into the field on the left and across to the gate on the far side.

Make your way up the hill, keeping to the right of the tree filled hollow, through the hedge at the top and down the next field to the stile at the bottom. Continue ahead, through the gap into a small field then across to the metal gate, out into the lane and turn right. As you cross the bridge you will see the bridleway on the left, signed Pulham 1 mile. Go through the gate and follow the well-trodden track, up and round the field, to the farm gate at the top. Simply follow the bridleway back up to the main road, walk across and turn left. After passing the telephone kiosk it is safer to cross the road and walk back to the pub along the pavement.

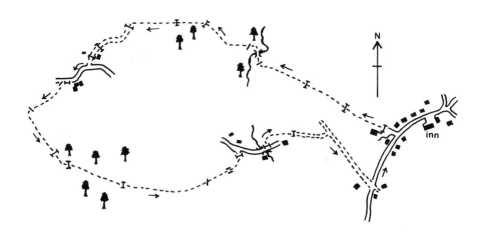

The Mitre Inn, Sandford Orcas

The Mitre Inn lies in the pretty village of Sandford Orcas. Three streams rise in the parish and in Saxon times the water was forded over a sandy bottom hence the name. The Manor House in the village became the property of a Norman family known as Orescuilz not an easy word for the locals to get their tongues round so it was simple called Orcas. From the front one enters directly into the hallway. On the right is a cosy dining area with an open fire and on the left the main bar which extends through to a room at the back with an inglenook open fireplace. There is also an additional dining area. The pub still has the original flag stone floor throughout and is comfortably but simply furnished in keeping with its age. At the back is a lawn beer garden where a barbecue area is being planned. The inn, a freehouse, changed hands as recently as 1990 and is personally run by the owners Mary and Ron with their daughter Sonya doing the cooking.

Two real ales include Courage Best and John Smiths Yorkshire Bitter.

The Mitre Inn is well known locally for its good food, it is all home-made and served seven days a week. A wide choice of bar snacks are available plus a full a la carte menu in the restaurant. For something different you can have escargot in garlic butter or fried breaded courgettes with a tzatziki dip. There are various steaks, whole lemon sole, roast duck, steak and kidney pie. Four appetizing vegetarian dishes include mushrooms, apples, raisins and peanuts in a parcel of filo pastry, served with grainy mustard sauce. On Sunday a special roast dinner can be ordered between 12 noon and 2 p.m. Daily specials are displayed on the blackboard in the bar.

Children are allowed in the inn and dogs if kept under control.

Opening times in the week are from 11 a.m. till 3 p.m. and 6.30 p.m. till 11 p.m.

The inn has three letting rooms.

Telephone: (0963) 22271.

The delightful little village of Sandford Orcas lies in hill country almost on the Dorset/Somerset border some three miles north of Sherborne, it is signed from the B3148.

Approx. distance of walk: 3 miles. O.S. Map No. 183 ST 626/205.

The inn has a small car park which is due to be extended. Parking is possible in the village road.

A short easy walk ideal for the whole family. It is mostly on very peaceful country lanes and tracks, and although dry for the most part, the track from Stafford's Green down towards Weathergrove Farm can become muddy when the weather is bad.

Turn right from the inn walking up the hill, past several houses, until you reach a signed footpath on the left close to a new house. Turn here, go through the gate and across the field to the gate in the far right-hand corner. Bear right and continue across the field to the gate in the far hedge, out on to the farm track and turn left. Continue through the farm, out to the lane, and turn left.

When you reach the road junction turn right, it is signed to Corton Denham, bearing left when you reach the road junction at Stafford's Green. After a while the lane narrows into a track which can become muddy when wet. At the bottom turn left following the lane, through the village, back to the pub.

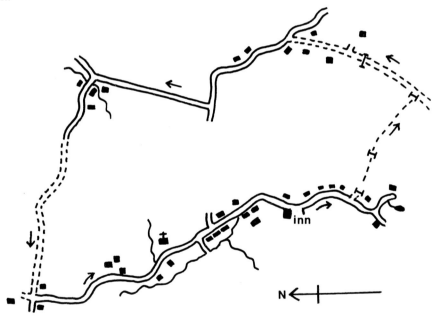

The sketch maps in this book are not necessarily to scale but have been drawn to show the maximum amount of detail.

The Drax Arms, Spettisbury

The present Drax Arms at Spettisbury was rebuilt after a fire in 1926 had destroyed the original thatched pub. The name is from the Drax Estate. Landowning families leased the pubs to the tenants and insisted that their arms be displayed for all to know who was the owner. Inside are two communicating bars, one with a dartboard, the other a more comfortable lounge. Outside seating is provided at the front and there is also a lawn beer garden at the side.

It is a Hall & Woodhouse inn serving one real ale Badger Best Bitter.

Good home-cooked bar food is available both lunch time and in the evening. Snacks include the usual sandwiches and ploughman's plus home-made soup. There is home-made steak and kidney pie, chilli and lasagne, various steaks and home-cooked ham.

The inn has no objection to children or dogs provided they are well behaved.

Opening times during the week are from 11 a.m. till 3 p.m. and from 6.30 p.m. till 11 p.m.

Telephone: (0258) 452658.

Walk No. 67

The Drax Arms is on the main A350, the Blandford side of the village.

Approx. distance of walk: 3½ miles. O.S. Map No. 195 ST 912/027.

The inn has its own car park at the rear. It is not safe to park in the road at the front.

A delightful scenic walk ideal for the whole family. It twice crosses the River Stour, takes you over Spettisbury Rings, an ancient Iron Age hill fort, and through the tiny hamlet of Tarrant Crawford. The going is fairly easy but parts can become muddy during bad weather.

From the pub turn right, walk across the road and up the short track signed to 'North Farm 1¼'. Cross the stile and head up the field. Go over another stile and cross the old railway bridge. After negotiating a second stile, the path rises to the top of the field. Keep close to the woods on the right, taking time as you go to look back and enjoy the view. When you reach a stile, leading off to the right, turn immediately left, into the field and walk across, bearing left, to a stile in the far corner. Go over, turn right, over another and bear left down the field making for the right-hand corner of a walled garden. Ahead of you is a stile and beyond a gate which brings you out onto a farm lane.

Turn right and go through the gate on the left, it is signed to 'Spettisbury Ring & Middle Buildings ¾'. Go up the slope to the top of the earthwork and walk round past the triangulation point. Follow the path down, and into the field, walking round beside the hedge, until you reach the stile which brings you out into the lane.

Turn left down to the crossroads and straight ahead, over the bridge, walking

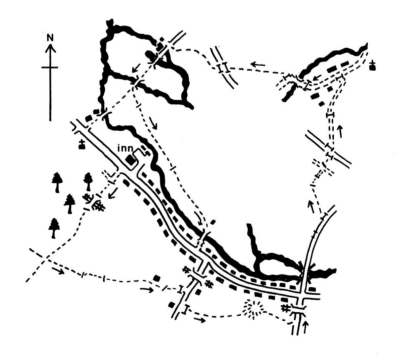

68

until you reach a small gate on the left. It is between two concrete posts and marked with a yellow arrow. Bear right across the field making for the electricity pylon. Go through both gates, under the pylon on to the track, over the stile and up the field ahead, then out through the gate into the road.

Walk straight across, through the gate and on to the bridleway. After a second gate the track leads down to meet the tarred lane at the bottom. Go through the small gate and turn left past farm buildings and Tarrant Abbey House. After crossing the small bridge, just beyond the entrance to the house, there is a farm gate on the right, it is waymarked. Go through into the field and bear left, over to the gate in the far hedge. Cross the road, go through the gate opposite and turn right, walking through the market garden leaving

the field opposite the farm shop and then turn left.

The footpath passes close to a house before a picturesque bridge takes you across the river into the field. Keep straight ahead, over another bridge. From here two routes take you back to the pub. You can either continue ahead, turning left when you reach the main road, or follow the route I prefer by turning left here and make for the wooden crossing point in the fence then bear right across the meadow. As you approach the river you will see a large yellow arrow on the distant telegraph pole marking the route. Keep walking in the same direction, over another crossing point, and make for a building close to the river. Go round to the right, then over the bridge, up the track to the main road and turn right along the pavement back to the pub. It is a fairly busy road so take care.

The Footbridge Across The River Stour

The Royal Oak Inn, Stour Provost

At first sight this village local could easily be mistaken for a private house. I was therefore not surprised to learn that it was once a girls school. Although the building itself dates back to the 18th-century it only became a pub around the turn of this century. The popular inn name refers to Charles' escape after the Battle of Worcester. There are two attractive bars both similarly furnished with a warm log fire. At the back is a large garden with views over the Stour.

It is a Hall & Woodhouse pub with Badger Best real ale.

Good reasonably priced food is available seven days a week. From the main menu a good choice of snacks include soup with granary bread, ploughman's, and sandwiches, plain and toasted. Jacket potatoes come with a choice of fillings such as garlic mushrooms topped with cheese, tuna fish, onion and mayonnaise. Also on the menu is home-cooked ham, cottage pie, gammon, lasagne, home-made chilli, a choice of omelettes and various burgers. Children have their own menu. Daily specials are chalked on the blackboard.

Families are welcome but dogs are only allowed in the garden.

Opening hours are from 11.30 a.m. till 3 p.m. (12 noon till 2.30 p.m. in the winter), and from 6 p.m. till 11 p.m.

Telephone: (0747) 85247.

Stour Provost is a small hamlet signed from the B3092 between Marnhull and East Stour about three miles south from Gillingham.

Approx. distance of walk: 4¼ miles. O.S. Map No. 183 ST 794/215.

The inn has a large car park at the back. Only limited parking is possible in the lanes by the pub.

An enjoyable walk mostly across open farm land which twice crosses the River Stour. It is not a demanding walk but it can be muddy in a few places.

From the pub turn left, then left again, walking past the cottages down to the end of the lane. Go up on to the track on the right of the house following it until you reach a short track down into the field on the left. Bear right across to the far corner, over the stream, heading in the same direction towards the bridge. On the far bank turn right, and after a few yards, head up the field towards the Ship Inn. Just before reaching the road you will see a stile on the right allowing access to the car park.

Cross the road and turn left. Cross back again when you reach a thatched cottage. There is a footpath running down beside the house, it is signed Fifehead Church ½. Keeping close to the hedge, walk down this path to the bottom of the garden, go over the stile into the field and make your way down to the bridge at the bottom. Cross into the field and go up to the pair of stiles. Keep straight ahead to the gap in the opposite hedge, go through and bear right, through the two metal kissing gates on either side of the grass track. Follow the path across to the stile and into the field ahead, over another stile and finally over one last stile into the road and turn left.

Almost opposite the telephone kiosk you will see a footpath, it is signed, Old Mill Marnhull ¾. It runs down beside the house to the bottom of the garden where there is a stile. Go into the field and straight ahead, keeping close to the hedge on the left. Continue through a gap in the hedge, down the field ahead, and cross the track walking down to the stile in the far hedge. Keep straight ahead over one more stile, go through the gate and bear right over to the bridge.

Cross into the field, go over the stile by the house and down the drive, turning left at the entrance. The footpath is signed, Stour Provost 1¼. Go over the stile into the field and turn right. Keeping fairly close to the hedge, continue ahead over a stile into another field. The path then follows the course of the river, through a gap into another field and eventually reaches a stile in the hedge beyond which is a ditch. Go across into the field and bear right up to the stile in the top hedge.

Cross the road and go over the stile into the field opposite. Bear left making for a stile in the far hedge then continue ahead, through the gate and over to a pair of stiles in the opposite hedge. Bear right across the field to a couple more stiles at the back of the barn then straight ahead over the stile in the wire fence. Make your way up to the gate by the hedge, go through, then bear left to one last crossing point at the back of a thatched cottage. Go down to the lane and turn right back to the pub.

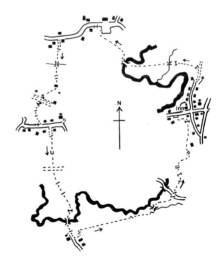

The sketch maps in this book are not necessarily to scale but have been drawn to show the maximum amount of detail.

The Springhead, Sutton Poyntz

An idea of a perfect summers evening, to many people, would be to sit outside a peaceful village pub, overlooking a duck pond, quenching their thirst with a cool drink. I have often done just that at The Springhead in Sutton Poyntz. This attractive little village was once home to the many local farm workers whose ancestors moved down from the surrounding hills after the departure of the Romans. It was an obvious place to live below the natural spring. The waters still flow forming the delightful, willow fringed pond in front of the inn.

The aptly named 'Springhead' is a Devenish Premier inn. It dates back to the turn of the century and was built from local stone. The imposing exterior giving the impression of an old manor house. Inside are two comfortable linked bars with a separate dining area at one end. The attractive interior has part panelled walls and a beamed ceiling. Additional heat is provided in the end bar by an open log fire. The whole area is carpeted throughout with an assortment of comfortable chairs and couches. Picnic benches are provided at the front and there is also a beer garden and children's play area at the rear.

Two real ales presently offered are Royal Wessex and Ruddles Bitter.

Good home-cooked food is available seven days a week. From the constantly changing menu in the winter there is hot soup, stews and pies whilst in the summer cold soups and salads. In addition there is always available the usual pub favourites like sandwiches and ploughman's.

Dogs are allowed and children when accompanied by parents.

During the summer the inn is open all day from 11 a.m. to 11 p.m. closing in the winter between 3 p.m. and 6 p.m.

Telephone: (0305) 832117.

A delightful village on the outskirts of Weymouth north of Preston. It is signed from the A353.

Approx. Distance of walk: 3½ miles. O.S. Map No. 194 SY 707/838.

The inn has a large car park at the side and rear plus a small area opposite, beside the pond.

A very scenic walk up to, and over, the well known White Horse Hill; best walked on a calm summers day. It is very hilly, steep in places and often very muddy especially in the winter.

Leave the inn and turn right and then right again on to the track, the footpath is signed. Go through the gate and straight ahead through three more then round the field, following a route fairly close to the hedge. Go through the little gate in the corner and straight across to the gate opposite, over the wooden crossing in the far hedge, and bear right to the gate opposite. It is often very muddy made worse by cattle movements. Make your way over the little stream and follow the path across the field to exit by the gate opposite the stone house.

Turn left on to the inland route of the Dorset coast Path. The track takes you to the top of White Horse Hill where you get a lovely panoramic view of Weymouth Bay. Go through the gate on the left in the direction of Bincombe. Keep to the main path, through a couple more gates, out to join a gravel track, and turn left. After passing a couple of tumuli, turn left through the gate by the derelict buildings. Further on, go through the gate on the right and walk round the meadow.

Before reaching the gate on the far side bear left down the hillside following the line of the telegraph poles. You will pick up a rough track which will take you to the bottom. Go through the gate on the right and follow the gravel track, through a couple of gates back to the pub.

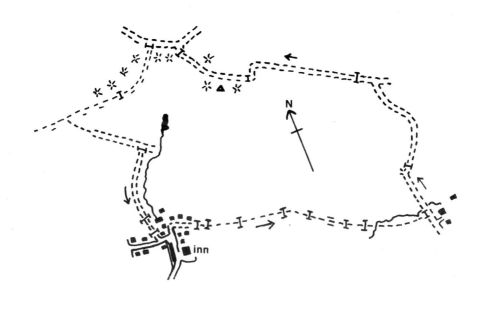

The sketch maps in this book are not necessarily to scale but have been drawn to show the maximum amount of detail.

The Bugle Horn, Tarrant Gunville

A mile and a half up the Tarrant Valley, from the main Salisbury to Blandford road, lies the peaceful village of Tarrant Gunville with its splendid pub the Bugle Horn. Looking more like a fine country house it is surrounded by trees and stands in its own ground overlooking fields. It is a freehouse very well run by the owners, Bernard and Lise Goswell who took over as recently as 1989. It is very much a village local. Inside are two cosy rooms served by the same bar, with a log fire in winter. Furnishings consist of comfortable chairs, tables and wooden settles. There is a large attractive beer garden at the rear and a small terrace at the front with tables and chairs.

The well stocked bars includes two real ales: the delightful Ringwood Bitter and Wadsworth 6X.

Freshly prepared food is available seven days a week. There are the usual pub snacks such as sandwiches, ploughman's, salads and basket meals. Also various steaks, a chicken curry and vegetarian meals like pizza. Two popular dishes are their own home-made steak pie and beef lasagne.

Children are welcome, if well behaved, the same goes for dogs.

The inn is open five days a week from 11.30 a.m. till 2.30 p.m. sometimes 3 o'clock and in the evening from 6 p.m. till 11 p.m. On Saturday the inn is open all day from 11 a.m. till 11 p.m.

Telephone: (025 889) 300

This peaceful Dorset village is easily reached from the A354 at Tarrant Hinton.

Approx. distance of walk: 5 miles. O.S. Map No. 195 ST 926/127.

There is plenty of parking space both at the front and beside the inn. You can also park in most of the side roads in the village.

A most enjoyable walk to the delightful hamlet of Chettle. It is mostly easy going along byways, bridle paths and across farm land.

Leave the pub and turn left, cross the road and go up the lane on the right. Near the top bear left and walk up towards a block of three garages. A short track leads up to a farm gate where a narrow path on the right passes behind the houses into the wood. Follow the path up through the gate and straight ahead across the field making for a stile in the far left-hand hedge, go over on to the track and turn right.

When you reach the tarred drive go over the stile into the field opposite and walk round, staying close to the hedge on the right. A stile allows access to the adjoining field. Keeping close to the hedge on the left, walk round then through the gap in the corner and along the track, turning right when you reach the gap in the field on the right. Walk down to the bottom, through the gate and keep straight ahead following the track across the meadow towards Chettle. As you enter the farmyard turn immediately right up the little path beside the tree. It brings you out into the lane opposite the church. Turn right.

The earliest record of a church on this site was in the 14th-century. Three bells, still in use, are now hung in the tower which was built in the early 16th-century. If you are in need of refreshment the small village post office would be happy to serve you.

Walk up the hill past Chettle House. If you wish to visit the House it is open from April till October every day, except Tuesday, from 10.30 a.m. till 5.30 p.m. The entrance fee to the house and gardens is currently £1.50. Ahead of you is a gate leading through to the bridle path. Ignore the path to the left but keep straight ahead, through another gate and then follow the grass path on the left, ignore the track ahead. When you reach a gate on the left go through and follow the track, eventually down to meet the road.

Turn left and cross the road then turn right up the stone track. Walk past the farm building turning right at the woods. Further ahead go through the gate and follow the narrow path between the woods and the field. On the far side a similar gate brings you onto a track which widens and joins with a tarred lane. Turn right at the junction back down to the village and right again back to the pub.

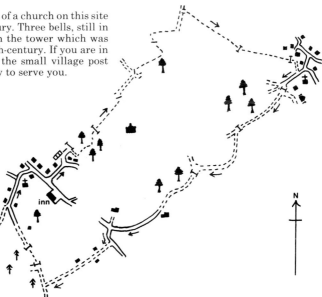

The Old Swan Inn, Toller Porcorum

Toller Porcorum is a delightful village in the heart of Dorset. The population in 1985 was only 239, since when it has greatly increased. The village name meaning (Toller of the Pigs) appears in the Doomsday Book as Tolre and was called Swynestolre. It is thought its name came from the vast number of pigs kept in the oak woods, or from the wild boar which where hunted by a succession of Kings in Powerstock Forest. This friendly village local was then aptly named The Old Swine but much later changed to the present Old Swan. Two inter-connected bars are both simply but comfortably furnished. One bar has a small piano the other a dartboard and bar billiards table. Additional heating is provided by a wood burning stove. There is a skittle alley at the back, a family room and a small beer garden.

The inn is owned by Palmers. From the well stocked bar there is one real ale, I.P.A. Bitter and occasionally Tally Ho. Also three different lagers and traditional cider.

A small but adequate food menu is available. There are sandwiches, plain and toasted, ploughman's, steak and kidney pie, mini pizzas, and a hot pasty or sausages with bread and butter.

Dogs are welcome on a lead and children in the family room.

The inn can offer overnight accommodation and has three letting rooms.

Opening times during the week are from 10.30 a.m. till 3 p.m. and from 6.30 p.m. till 11 p.m.

Telephone: (0300) 20391.

Village signed off the A356, Dorchester to Crewkerne road.

Approx. distance of walk: 4¾ miles. O.S. Map No. 194 563/979.

Park at the back of the pub, or at the front in 'High Street', near the village shop.

The water meadows around Toller Porcorum often make walking difficult and extremely muddy so a large part of our walk is directed along the surrounding country lanes. They are very peaceful with very little traffic. The best time is early spring when the hedgerows are draped with a colourful mantle of wild flowers. The walk is very enjoyable, and apart from the mud, is fairly easy going.

Start by walking down Kingcombe Lane beside the inn, it is signed to Hook. After passing several houses turn right onto the bridleway, signed Lower Kingcombe ¾. Walk round and through the gate into Manor Farm. Leave through the gate at the back and continue along the track then through the gate into the field. Go straight across to pick up the track beyond the gate in the hedge opposite, it can sometimes be quite muddy. In Spring it is dotted with many wild flowers including numerous primroses. At one point, where the track veers right, you will see a stile straight ahead of you. You can either keep to the track or cut across the field and meet the track again on the far side. Ignore the bridleway from the right but continue following the track to join the lane at Lower Kingcombe.

Turn left and cross the river walking past The Kingcombe Centre. On the right is a wooden farm gate, it is waymarked. Go into the field and across, bearing slightly to the left. To help you there are Waymarker posts showing the path. After a short distance the path veers right, down across the river and into the field. Turn left and make for the gap in the thicket, cross the stile and ditch, then bear right, up and across the field to the stile set in the hedge opposite. Continue ahead, through the gate and over to the stile. Walk beside the pond towards the farm then straight ahead, out through the farm gate opposite and along the lane, turning left at the crossroads.

The walk continues along peaceful country lanes for about 2½ miles. The hedgerows can be a picture with masses of wild flowers. When I last walked here I watched a young rabbit being chased continually up and down the lane by a weasel. When you reach the road junction turn left, it is signed 'Toller Porcorum'. Bear right at the junction walking down past woodland to the bottom of the hill. As you pass under the old railway bridge you will see a gate on the left, the path is signed. Go through, and bear right across the field to the gate in the far right-hand hedge. Turn left, cross the stream, and gully, go over the crossing point and into the field. The path is easy to follow passing through several fields and over a wooden crossing point before a gate gives access into one last field. Keep close to the hedge on the left, out through the gate, into the lane and turn left back to the pub.

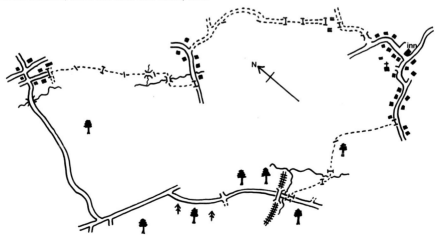

The Rose & Crown Inn, Trent

Situated overlooking fields beside a farm in the ancient village of Trent is the lovely Rose & Crown, initially formed by two separate thatched cottages, the present front joined them together in about 1720. The inn was originally a farmhouse with a licence to sell alcohol. Once the last of the cattle departed in the 1950's it became a full pub and has remained independent ever since. From the lovely flag stoned entrance hall a family room leads off to the right and the main bar to the left. It has a tiled floor, simple chairs, tables and high back wooden settles with a warm log fire. A small room off the bar, originally the office, has a lovely old inglenook fireplace found only recently during decorating. The most recent addition is a delightful conservatory dining room.

Being a freehouse a good range of real ale is available. Oakhill Brewery across the border in Somerset was set up by a farmer in 1984. Its two delightful beers are sold in the pub, Oakhill Bitter, often still known as Farmers, and the strong Yeoman's Ale. There is also Exmoor Ale, Butcombe Bitter and Smiles.

In 1986 the present licensees, Chas and Nancy Marion-Crawford, took over the pub bringing with them a lifetime experience in cooking. There is a good choice of bar snacks available all week except Friday and Saturday nights and Sunday lunch times. You can have smoked Scottish salmon, imported French seafood soup with rouilles and garlic bread. Main meals include 'Croque Monsieur' – gammon, pineapple and melted cheese on two slices of hot toast, a Yankee cheese steak sandwich, spicy chicken wings and the chef's choice of a curry. Daily specials might include spinach and gruyer cheese en croute, Mediterranean whitefish Provincial, roast pheasant and supreme of chicken in garlic cream.

The inn is open daily from 12 noon till 2.30 p.m. and from 7 p.m. (6.30 p.m. during June, July and August) till 11 p.m.

Telephone: (0935) 850776.

Trent, a small village close to the county border, is signed from the B3148 north west of Sherborne.

Approx. distance of walk: 2¾ miles. O.S. Map No. 183 ST 591/185.

Park outside the inn or in the field at the side.

A short walk over farmland and along peaceful country lanes, ideal for a summers evening. Although easy going it can be muddy in places during wet weather.

From the inn go back to the road and turn right. Walk past the church and turn left into the wide gravel drive. After passing the end wall of the church, where the drive bears right, look for a gap in the hedge on the left and follow the path through the shrubbery. The last time I walked this path the route to the bottom had become overgrown and a wooden crossing point had been provided leading into the field on the left; this is the route I had to take. If you find the same problem I suggest you do likewise. Once in the field turn right and walk to the bottom.

Exit through the gate, walk across the road and through the gate opposite. The path bears right across the field to the farm gate. Go through on to the track, cross over the bridge, down the far side and through the gate into the field on the right. Walk over to the far hedge, go through the gate and bear left across to the corner of the field. There you will find a small bridge, cross the stream and bear left making for the point where the hedge boundary meets a wire fence, the path is marked. Go through into the field ahead, bear right and leave by the gap in the top hedge, out on to the track and turn right, it is signed.

When you reach the lane turn right, walk over the bridge and take the turning on the left signed to Trent. At the road junction continue ahead towards Adber, past some farm buildings, and take the lane on the right. Walk down to the road junction, turn right and then left into Mill Lane. Continue along the lane passing the cottage on the right. A short distance further on you will see a signed footpath on the right leading up into a field. Make your way across in the direction of the church bearing left to the back of the pub. A stile, conveniently situated, allows access directly to the front entrance.

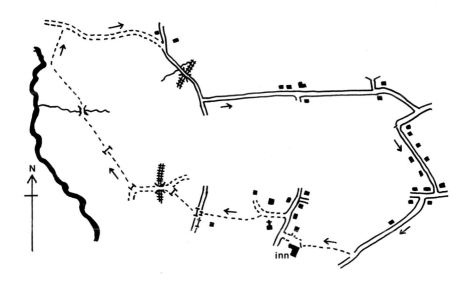

The Riverside Inn, Tuckton

For many years the Riverside Inn was one of my favourite pubs, not least for its magnificent riverside setting. I still like it but today it is more commercial. It is a Roast Inn, part of the Whitbread chain, the original bars at the front are now knocked into one and a new restaurant extension added at the back. The excellent restaurant, set on various levels including one section with views over the River Avon, is beautifully and imaginatively decorated throughout. Outside on the river bank are a number of picnic benches. You can even hire a boat.

Two real ales are served from handpump: Marston's Pedigree and Strong Country Bitter.

For those wishing to eat, you have the choice of a carvery meal in the restaurant or a snack in the bar. All hot food is home-made on the premises. Apart from ploughman's and salads, each day there are dishes listed on the blackboard such as turkey hot pot, barbecue spicy chicken wings and ribs, braised beef, turkey curry, sweet and sour gammon and turkey a la king. All dishes come with the option of rice or french fries with veg or salad. If you wish to eat in the restaurant it is best to book. Food is served during the week between 12 noon and 2 p.m. and from 6 p.m. till 10 p.m. Sunday from noon till 3.30 p.m. and 6 p.m. to 9.45 p.m. You have the choice of a two or three course meal with special meals for children.

Between Monday and Friday an area in the restaurant is set aside for families with children not wishing to eat. Dogs are not allowed inside the pub.

Opening times can be flexible but at the moment, the pub is open all day, between Monday and Friday, from 11 a.m. till 11 p.m. and Saturday from 11 a.m. till 3.30 or 4.30 p.m. and again from 5.30 p.m. until 11 p.m.

Telephone: (0202) 429210.

The pub is beside Tuckton Bridge on the banks of the Avon on the B3059.

Approx. distance of walk: 5 miles. O.S. Map No. 195 SZ 148/923.

Park at the pub, in Wick Lane or in the public car park by the river.

An extremely enjoyable walk for the whole family. Hengistbury Head, with its salt marshes, is the last vestige for wildlife in the Bournemouth – Christchurch conurbation. The walk takes you through Wick village to the top of the Head, down to the shore and back through a nature trail and along the bank of the river.

From the pub cross the road and walk down Wick Lane. If you bear left down to the riverside park a tarred path runs parallel with the lane ending in Wick Village. Ignore the sign directing you to the Head but keep straight ahead and follow the lane round to the right and out into Harbour Road. Turn left along the front of the school, past the pitch and putt course and round to meet the road. Walk straight across and make your way over the grass to the cliff path.

Many walks cross the Head including a circular nature trail. Our walk combines the best of both. Keep to the path by the shore. When you reach the Head walk up the steps to the top and take the path on the right past the Coast Guard Lookout Station.

After rounding the headland go down the steps to the beach and along the track behind the beach huts. At the turning point for the 'Noddy Train' go left following the shore line, over the wooden crossing points and back to meet the tarred road. If the weather is very bad, or in times of extremely high tides, keep to the tarred road.

After you pass the wardens house turn right, signed to Wick village. Go through the gate and into the field on the left. If you keep close to the fence the path will take you round beside the reed beds; a feeding and resting area for many migrating birds. It is also a good spot to pick blackberries.

Go through the gate and cross the bridge, then through the kissing gate and keep straight ahead making for the right-hand corner of the converted farm buildings. The path veers to the right through a couple more gates before reaching the river bank. This time simply follow the path beside the river which will take you straight back to the pub.

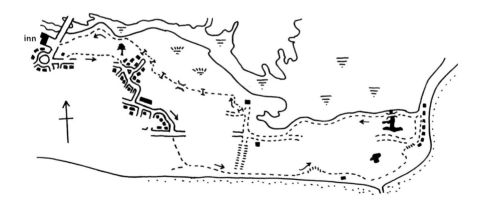

The sketch maps in this book are not necessarily to scale but have been drawn to show the maximum amount of detail.

The Albion Inn, Verwood

The name Albion refers to the ancient name for Britain, it is of Celtic origin. This friendly family run pub though is not that old. It was built at the same time as the railway in 1866. Pictures of how the original pub looked in those days can be seen hanging around the walls. After the railway was closed and the line ripped up the pub was refurbished and a beer garden with chairs tables and picnic benches was added. The attractive main bar is comfortably furnished with padded wall settles. Above the part wood panelled walls are a large number of brightly shining brass and copper items. A small area behind the chimney is kept as a dining area where tables can be booked. There is a separate public bar with a warm log fire and a small room off the main bar.

The inn is owned by Gibbs Mew, a family brewery established in 1856 and still independent. Two well conditioned real ales are available: Salisbury Best and the delightful but very strong Bishop's Tipple. The East Dorset branch of CAMRA voted it their pub of the year in 1990.

Good reasonably priced food is served seven days a week including a Sunday roast. The landlord's wife Mavis does the cooking and very good it is too. Freshly prepared snacks include salads, ploughman's, sandwiches and rolls. There are home-made dishes such as a tasty curry, chilli and a popular speciality – spare ribs. I can personally vouch for those. In the evening there is a more extensive menu. From the list of starters there are mussels in garlic butter. Main meals include various fish dishes, grills, duck a la orange, venison in red wine and veal in a creamy mushroom and garlic sauce. Each day there is a special which could be 'chicken Italian', chicken cooked with peppers, onions, tomatoes and white wine. Dogs are not allowed.

The inn is open during the week from 11 a.m. till 2.30 p.m. and from 5 p.m. (6 p.m. on Saturday) till 11 p.m.

Telephone: (0202) 825267.

The inn is situated on the B3081, west from the village centre.

Approx. distance of walk: 4¼ miles. O.S. Map No. 195 SU 076/094.

Park beside the inn or in the old road at the back.

An enjoyable country walk which takes you across farm land and through bluebell woods to the village of Edmondsham. The going is fairly easy but some paths can become muddy in places.

Turn right from the inn along the B3061, cross the bridge and turn left when you reach West Farm, the path is waymarked. Follow the track past several cottages and through a couple of gates. Further along the track you will see a gate on the right, the footpath is signed into the field crossing diagonally to the far corner. When I last did the walk there was a notice requesting one to carry along the track for a further hundred yards or so, and then turn into the field keeping close to its southern boundary which seems more sensible.

A well defined path from the top corner takes you up past Mount Pleasant Farm on to a gravel drive. Further ahead take the turning on the right, walking past various properties before reaching the lane. Go straight across, down the grass path opposite and over the crossing point behind the rear of a private garden. After another crossing point a short path brings you into an open grass area. Bear left to pick up the path again walking down past the house into the road.

At the bottom go through the gate on the

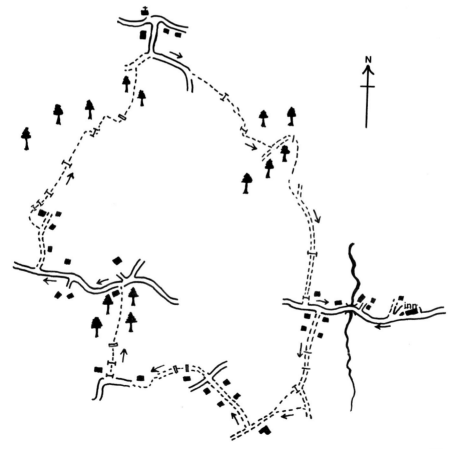

right next to Whitemore House and through a second gate into the field. Keeping close to the fence walk to the far side and cross the ditch into the bluebell wood. The path is fairly straightforward but does become muddy in bad weather. When you reach the road turn left. Although not a very busy road it carries some fast traffic at times so a little care is necessary.

Continue round a couple of bends, up the hill, turning right into the gravel drive, it is signed 'Edmondsham 1'. Just before reaching a corrugated roofed building and almost opposite a bungalow, turn left across an area of grass towards the hedge then bear right behind the building. After several gates you reach a field. Continue across, through a gate into a larger field walking to the far right-hand corner. Go through the gate and turn left keeping close to the hedge, round past the corner of the field and then over the wooden crossing point into the wood on the left. Follow the well defined path to the track at the bottom, turn right,

then right again when you reach the road, unless of course you want to visit Edmondsham House.

Continue along the lane only as far as the first bend then go through the gap in the hedge on the left, across the field and through the gate on the far side. Bear right walking up to and through the gap in the hedge opposite then make your way to the gate in the far top corner of the field. Go through and turn left. Keep close to the hedge, until you reach the brow of the hill. At this point bear right and walk across to the far corner of the field into the wood, it is waymarked. A few steps further on follow the path to the left, through the woods to the far side. Go over the crossing point and bear right across the field, through the gap in the hedge, across to another gap in the hedge on the left, then out on to a farm track. Turn right passing through a couple of farm gates before reaching the road then turn left back to the inn.

Hardy's Monument, walk no. 63

George III on the White Horse
walk no. 69

The view from Hengistbury Head
walk no. 73

The Quay Inn, Wareham

Facing south, overlooking the Frome, this delightful pub was originally three cottages. Later the end cottages became two pubs and eventually combined with the middle cottage to form one large pub known as the New Inn. It was later renamed The Quay Inn. There are two bars simply but attractively furnished each with a large open fireplace, one having a warm log fire. Overlooking the quay there is a sunny terrace with picnic benches and a secluded walled beer garden at the back.

The well stocked bar has an interesting wine list and a choice of real ales: Flowers Original, Marstons Pedigree and Boddingtons Bitter and for the winter, Wethereds Winter Royal.

A very good menu, including vegetarian meals, is available, both lunchtime and in the evening, seven days a week. Snacks include home-made soup, ploughman's, salads, home-made garlic bread and jacket potatoes with ten different fillings. Speciality pies are a local favourite. 'Wareham Pie' is half an oval pie dish of steak and kidney cooked in Guinness the other half filled with cauliflower cheese and topped with puff pastry. 'Poole Pie' has smoked fish and shellfish in a creamy parsley sauce and 'New Forest Game Pie' is a rich mixture of game, wild forest mushrooms and black cherries cooked in the pubs own recipe stock laced with mead. Also available are a range of grills, half a rack of lamb and even a whole roast hock in a cider and apple sauce. Each day there are several specials listed on the blackboard plus a daily roast. To complete your meal there are several tempting sweets such as Dorset cider apple cake and cherry special, home-made shortbread with real dairy cream.

Children are welcome if eating with their parents in the restaurant bar.

During the summer the pub is open Monday through till Saturday from 10.30 a.m. till 11 p.m. The inn can also offer overnight accommodation and has three letting rooms.

Telephone: (0929) 552735.

Walk No. 75

The Quay Inn, as its name would imply, is on the quay at Wareham on the Swanage side of the A351.

Approx. distance of walk: 4 miles. O.S. Map No. 195 SY 924/873.

The pub does not have its own car park but public parking is allowed on the quay itself, tickets to be obtained from a meter. There is another car park in the square near the church.

A most enjoyable river side walk ideal for a warm summers evening or a cold winters day. It is fairly flat, easy going and mostly dry underfoot although care is necessary on the path by the river as the surface can be a bit uneven in places. The only unsuitable time would be during an exceptionally high river; some parts of the path are quite low and liable to become waterlogged.

Turn left from the pub and go through the gap between the houses up to the church. Walk past the front of the church, and the entrance to the graveyard, and along the lane turning right when you reach Wyatts Lane. Go down to the bottom, then round to the left and up the bank onto Town Walls. Further on the path dips down to meet a road from the left. At this point turn right across the lane and go up the concrete farm entrance, the path is signed, go through the farm gate and straight ahead along the track.

It is quite long and eventually merges with a footpath. After crossing three stiles you reach Swineham Point. Simply follow the raised river bank footpath as it snakes its way through the reeds round the head-land and back along the river edge towards the town. As you near the church the path veers right down some steps and through the reed beds. Continue following the path round, past a house and over a stile onto a well established footpath. At the end of the path go over the stile turning left through the gate and up to the road.

Turn left. When you reach the crossroads, go up the grass bank onto East Walls, along the top and down to the lane. Keep straight ahead taking the right turn through the cemetery, round to the church and back to the pub.

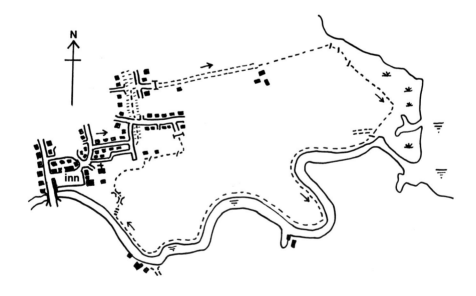

Hare & Hounds, Waytown

Throughout West Dorset there are many small peaceful hamlets well off the beaten track going about their business in their own unhurried way. Most have their own village pub which is more than just a place to drink, it is the centre of village life. The Hare & Hounds in Waytown is one such pub. There is just one main bar selling everything from beer to winter mixture. It is simply furnished and heated by a warm coal stove. A small door at the side leads down to a cosy parlour which is in fact the dining room. Lots of gleaming brass and copper items adorn the walls. Outside there is a large front lawn with picnic benches. Upstairs is an interesting antiquarian library which brings people from far and wide looking for special titles.

It is a Palmers House serving two real ales. Their Best Bitter and I.P.A.

Very reasonably priced food is served seven days a week, the majority of it being home-made. There are snacks such as soup with hot bread, ploughman's and tasty pies of chicken and mushroom or beef with stilton. The menu offers a choice of grills and four curry dishes. Lunch and dinner dishes include chicken casserole, braised liver, boiled ham with dumplings, smoked haddock, beef stew and a roast of the day. Daily specials listed on the blackboard might offer a tasty pork and pineapple casserole. A good choice of sweets include treacle tart and apple pie.

Opening times are from 11 a.m. till 2 p.m. and from 6 p.m. till 11 p.m.

Families are welcome and dogs if kept under control.

Telephone: (03088) 203.

Walk No. 76

Waytown lies well off the beaten track west of the Britt river between Bridport and Beaminster. Take the turning signed to 'Waytown & Oxbridge' from the A3065.

Approx. distance of walk: 3¼ miles. O.S. Map 193 SY 470/978.

The inn has its own car park.

An enjoyable walk in this peaceful part of rural Dorset. It follows the course of the River Britt, through Netherbury and Oxbridge, along quiet country lanes, on bridleways and over farm land. It is fairly easy going but muddy in places during bad weather.

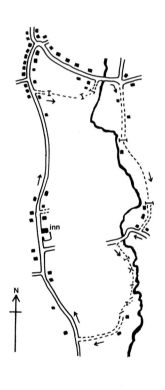

Leave the pub and turn right along the lane towards Netherbury. As you approach the village, but before reaching a lane on the left, look for a signed footpath on the right beside a cottage, 'The Old Malthouse'. Go through the gate then over the stile into the field and follow the path round to the left. Continue through a couple more gates, on to a drive, out into the road and turn right. Alternatively, if you prefer, you can keep to the lane turning right when you reach the village centre.

Cross the bridge and turn right up the track. It is a bridle path so be prepared for it to be muddy in the winter. When you reach the weir go through the large farm gate into the field and straight ahead, keeping fairly close to the hedge on the right. A gate further ahead allows access to a short track which takes you down to meet the lane at Oxbridge.

Turn right, cross the bridge and go over the stile set in the hedge on the left. Continue ahead, keeping fairly close to the river, through a gate into the field ahead, then across a ditch, over the stile and ahead to the wooden crossing point. In the hedge opposite is a stile. Go over, then immediately right, through a small gate, up the bank and bear left across the field to the stile in the corner. Follow the track round to meet the lane turning right back to the inn.

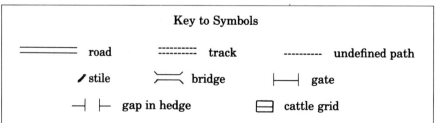

Key to Symbols

═══════ road	┈┈┈┈ track	┈┈┈┈ undefined path
✔ stile	⟩══⟨ bridge	├──┤ gate
┤ ├ gap in hedge	⊟ cattle grid	

The sketch maps in this book are not necessarily to scale but have been drawn to show the maximum amount of detail.

New Inn, West Knighton

What was once a row of farm cottages, some two to three hundred years ago, is today a popular village local. One end is devoted to pub games the other a comfortable restaurant area with the main bar in the centre. There is also a skittle alley, a large beer garden and children's play area at the rear overlooking fields.

There are two Devenish real ales: J. D. Dry Hop and Vallence's Bitter.

The present licensees, Roger and Julia Gilbey, took over the lease four years ago and are steadily building a reputation for good home-cooked food. It is all freshly prepared to order. The set menu includes bar meals of lasagne, cauliflower cheese, omelettes, ploughman's, jacket potatoes, home-made soup, sandwiches and a vegetarian fruit and nut pilaf. Also steak and a rack of spare ribs. Daily specials are chalked on the board in the bar. Dishes such as beef curry, calamaris, home-baked vegetarian quiche and deep fried mushrooms. Sometimes there is even an extra specials board which might offer Grandma Batty's huge Yorkshire pudding filled with turkey fricassee in white wine sauce or beef in Guinness with broccoli.

Weekday opening times are from 11 a.m. till 2.30 p.m. and from 7 p.m. till 11 p.m.
Children are welcome. Dogs too but only in the bar if kept under control.
Overnight accommodation is available in one self contained room.
Telephone: (0305) 852349.

Walk No. 77

The village is signed from Broadmayne about three miles east of Dorchester on the main A352 road to Wool

Approx. distance of walk 3¼ miles: O.S. Map No. 194 733/878.

The pub has a small parking area at the front and a larger car park through the archway at the back. The main village street is fairly narrow but it is possible to park near the telephone kiosk, or in the small layby at the bottom of the hill near the start of the walk.

An interesting scenic walk through woods, over streams and across farm land, ideal for a warm summer's evening. The going is fairly easy although can be very muddy in the winter.

Leave the inn and turn left. At the bottom of the hill turn right on to the concrete drive leading to Empool Pumping Station. Bear left at the top, the drive ahead leads to the pumping station and is not a public right of way. Continue round a couple of bends until the track dips towards the quarry entrance. On the right is a farm gate. Go through, and straight ahead following the track past the old barn and along the valley bottom. As you approach the wood bear right up to the gate, go through, and turn left. The path runs between the edge of the wood and the field to the corner by the pylon. Go through the gate and turn right.

The narrow track skirts the top of the quarry before dividing in two directions. Take the right fork down to the watercress farm, walk between the buildings, cross the stream and go up the gravel track ahead. A short distance ahead a track crosses at right angles, turn right here. The track passes through woodland before reaching a short

track on the right leading down to the stream. Take this track then cross the stream turning right by the thatched cottage. The path is signed to West Knighton. Climb over the wooden crossing point, cross the ditch, which can be tricky if the water level is high, go into the field and turn left.

Keeping close to the hedge, walk round the field, over a couple of crossing points, and across two more fields until you reach a double crossing point. Here bear right up the field following the waymarkers in the centre. Leave the field at the far top corner and turn left along the track and straight ahead into the field. Continue in the same direction, still following the waymarks, towards the stile in the far hedge. The little path runs between two private dwellings down to a cul-de-sac. Turn right following the path between the stone cottages, turning right again when you reach the village centre, back to the pub.

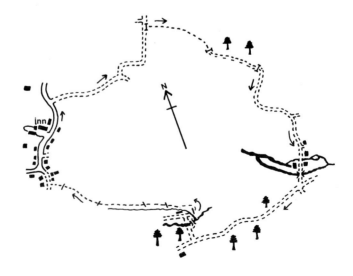

Five Bells Inn, Whitchurch Canonicorum

Throughout Dorset there are many simple village pubs, not necessarily smart, but comfortable friendly places where locals and tourists alike can meet in a relaxed atmosphere, enjoy a pint of well kept real ale and savour genuine local home-cooking. The Five Bells Inn is one such pub. Tucked peacefully away in this delightful little village it sits in its own grounds of 6½ acres. From the front it looks more like a family house. Two rooms lead off from the central entrance. On the left is the family room with an open log fire and on the right is the one simply furnished bar. Outside there are picnic benches, a children's play area and a pets corner.

It is a Palmers pub serving two real ales and draught Taunton Cider.

Good home-cooked food is available seven days a week. An amusing rider on the menu states that 'the management accept no responsibilty for meals unobtainable due to their own incompetence'. Snacks include ploughman's, salads, burgers and sandwiches, both plain and toasted; if you cannot find a filling you want from the menu you are invited to invent your own! Interestingly if you order a main meal you have the choice of a large or small portion. There are simple meals such as egg and chips and venison sausages, also steak and kidney pie, chilli, moussaka, lasagne, shepherd's pie, a choice of curries, tandoori chicken and steak and chips. For vegetarians there is vegetable lasagne and a nut roast. Other 'home-made things on the menu' rat soup with granary bread! 'we only use organically raised vegetarian rats'! Omelettes of cheese, ham, mushroom, hedgehog, tuna, whale or, as usual, anything else.

The pub has its own caravan and camping site and can offer overnight accommodation.

Opening times can be flexible especially in the summer months.

Telephone: (0297) 89262.

Walk No. 78

Although remotely situated the village is easily reached from the A3052, west of Bridport, at Morcombelake. The pub is on the Ryall road.

Approx. distance of walk 4¾ miles. O.S. Map No. 193 SY 397/954.

There is a large parking area beside the inn.

A lovely scenic walk in one of the most beautiful and peaceful parts of West Dorset. At first along country lanes, then through woods and across farm land, and finally back to the pub along the banks of the River Char. It is a hilly walk but not over demanding.

Leave the pub and walk down to the centre of the village. When you reach the crossroads turn right on to the Wootton Fitzpaine road. Cross the river and continue to the top of the hill until you reach Baker's Cross. On the left is a signed bridleway to 'Catherston 1¼'. Go up the narrow path, through the gate and around the field, keeping as close as possible to the hedge on the left and through the gate into the woods. Pausing occasionally to admire the view, follow the path up to the gate at the top. Keep straight ahead across the field, out through the gate, over the track, and through the gate opposite. On the right you have a good view of the Manor House, and ahead the sea at Charmouth.

Look for a gate in the hedge on the left, then go down the field making your way across to the hedge on the right. After a number of stiles you reach the river. Turn left and follow the bank until a bridge takes you to the other side. Walk up the track for a short distance then go over the stile on the

left, it is marked. After crossing another stile, and ditch, the path follows the course of the river through the meadow for some distance before a waymarked post directs you down to the river bank. Follow the signs, through the gate and continue along the meadow until you reach a little bridge over a tributary. Cross over and turn right heading up the field making for the wooden crossing point beside the large oak at the top.

Cross the lane, go over the stile and up the field to the stile in the corner. Continue ahead making for a gate in the opposite hedge. Go through and continue in the same direction, crossing the stile in the hedge, then bear left, through the farm gate, across the field, and through another gate in the hedge opposite. Make your way to the side of the farm, go out into the lane and turn right. Take the next turning on the left walking down to the village then turn right back to the pub.

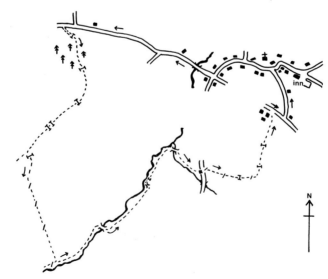

The Greyhound Inn, Winterborne Kingston

Until quite recently The Greyhound Inn was owned by Hall & Woodhouse the Blandford brewers. Today it is freehouse and very much a locals pub well run by the owners, Margaret and Ian Thorne. Alterations carried out by them include the addition of a new comfortable carvery restaurant. The main bar, remaining more or less unchanged, is comfortably furnished with a fireplace at one end. There is also a public bar and a skittle alley. Outside there is a beer garden and children's play area.

The well stocked bar includes two real ales Badger Best and Wadsworth 6X.

Good home-cooked food is available seven days a week. You can choose to eat from the generous help yourself carvery or from the bar menu. Snacks include ploughman's, salads, soup, home-made curry, chilli and filled jacket potatoes. There is a good choice of grilled and fried fish plus a wide selection of steaks from 'Diane' to a 24oz. T-bone. You can also have chicken kiev, roast chicken and a mixed grill. There is a separate children's menu and three vegetarian dishes. The tempting sweet menu includes home-made fruit pie and Dorset apple cake.

Children are welcome in the pub and dogs are allowed in the public bar if kept under control.

Overnight accommodation is available in en-suite bedrooms.

Normal weekday opening times are from 11 a.m. till around 2.30 p.m. and again from 6.30 p.m. till 11 p.m.

Telephone: (0929) 471332.

Walk No. 79

The village is signed from the A31, a short distance east from Bere Regis. It can also be reached from the north on the A354 Blandford to Puddletown road.

Approx. distance of walk 5 miles. O.S. Map No. 194 SY. 862/977.

The inn has its own car park. Limited parking is also available in the road at the front.

An easy going country walk mostly along bridleways, tracks and across farmland.

From the inn turn right along the main road walking only as far as the village shop. Cross the road and go down the lane towards the church. A short path at the side brings you into the lane. Turn right and then left into East Street. Continue down towards Abbot's Court Farm and go through the farm gate on the right. Keeping close to the hedge, follow the track around the field and out through the farm gate on the far side. Keep straight ahead on the gravel track until it bears left at which point go through the gate into the field on the right, it is signed. Continue across keeping close to the hedge, through a gap into the field ahead and finally out through a gate on to the bridleway and turn left.

The track rises gradually for some distance, then flattens towards fields. Sheep gates are often positioned along the path. Continue ahead until one last gate allows access into a small wood. Like many others in the area this wood suffered badly during the severe January storm of 1990. Go through to the far side and turn left when you reach the wire fence. A narrow path runs between the wood and the fence eventually leading out through a gate onto a gravel track.

Turn left and keep straight ahead into the field walking down to the metal gate at the bottom, go through and bear right, over the brow of the field to a stile set in the far right-hand hedge. Continue ahead through a gate and up the track. After passing some farm buildings you will see a wooden crossing point in the hedge on the left. Go into the field and bear right, walking in the direction indicated by the arrow across to the corner of the wood. Go over another crossing point and walk round the field, keeping close to the wood on the left, out through the gate on the far side onto the track and turn left.

Almost immediately on the right is a stile, go into the field and bear left, following the well worn path over two more crossing points and a small bridge. Continue across to one last fence then follow the path out into a cul-de-sac and turn right. Walk down Broad Close and then take the little path beside the bridge back to the pub.

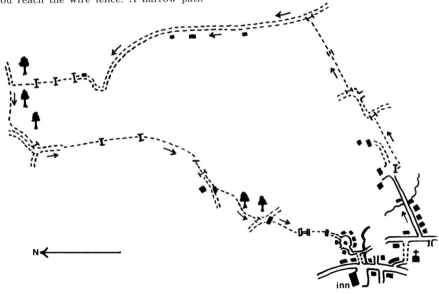

N ←————————

The Shire Horse, Winterborne Stickland

Originally called The Crown, The Shire Horse changed hands in 1990 and renamed. Its new owners, Hughen and Joyce Riley, who are no strangers to the licensed trade having previously run the Worlds End Pub, immediately set about the task of creating a typical village pub acceptable for both local and visitors alike. There is one main low beamed bar with brick, flint and plaster walls. At one end is an attractive inglenook fireplace with a warm open log fire. There are cottage type tables, chairs and window seats. Behind the main bar is the cosy dining room also with its own open fireplace and log fire. Meals are served on scrubbed pine farmhouse tables. Joyce's love of flowers is much in evidence, every table having a small display of fresh flowers. At the back is a courtyard with white plastic tables and chairs. The original well is still there but safely covered with a wire grill, also at the back is a raised grass bank with picnic benches and a children's play area.

Two real ales are served from handpumps: John Smith's Yorkshire Bitter and Courage Directors Bitter.

Hughen, a trained chef, presides over the kitchen to ensure all food is of the highest standard. Ploughman's are a speciality with six to choose from. Even the triple deck sandwiches can be a meal in themselves. Other pub favourites on the menu include home-made soup, jacket potatoes and home-made steak and kidney pie. An a la carte menu is available offering ten starters alone including scallops and bacon in a cream sauce. There is a good choice of steaks which come with the option of one of Hughen's delicious sauces. Also half a honey roast duck and a rack of lamb. The 'Chef's Special' is chicken breast filled with pate, bacon and avocado, wrapped in filo pastry and served with a green pepper sauce. Vegetarians are well catered for with four tasty dishes. There is also a children's selection. Weekly opening times are from 11 a.m. till 3 p.m. and 6.30 p.m. till 11 p.m.

Telephone: (0258) 880838.

Walk No. 80

The village is best reached from the A354 Blandford to Puddletown road at Winterborne Whitechurch. If you are coming from the north take the Okeford Fitzpaine road from the A357 at Shillingstone.

Approx. distance of walk 5 miles. O.S. Map No. 194 ST 835/046.

The pub has its own car park but one can park quite safely in the road at the front.

An enjoyable walk across fields to the hamlet of Winterborne Houghton, through Charity Wood then along bridleways and across open farm land back to the pub. Although hilly at times it is easy going but can become muddy in places in wet weather.

Leave the inn and turn right, cross the road and go up the short stony track beside Little Stickland Cottage. Go over the stile and bear left following the well walked track across the field behind the rear gardens of the houses. Cross the stile and continue ahead, keeping close to the lane, until you reach a farm gate then go through, down to the lane and turn right.

Turn left when you reach the track leading to St. Andrew's Church. The gravel drive bears left past the church before crossing the cattle grid on the far side. Continue up the slope and through the gate into the farmyard. On the left is a grassy bank. The footpath is not very well defined but you will see a blue arrow on the post. Go up the bank at this point then through the gate into the field and bear right keeping close to the hedge. At the top of the field go through the gate by the house and follow the narrow fenced path round the garden and out into the lane.

Walk straight across and through the metal gate opposite (the one on the right). Keeping close to the hedge, walk to the far side of the field and through the metal gate into the woods. Some distance ahead the path joins another from the right, turn left at this point, and a short distance further on, go over the stile into the field and walk straight across bearing left towards a gate in the far hedge. Do not go through but turn right and walk to the bottom of the field and across the stile and bridge out into the lane.

Walk straight across and up the gravel track beside the house. Go through the gate and straight ahead through the gate into the enclosed field. Keep to the fence walking round the field to the far side and then up the hill until you reach the farm gate on the right. Go through into the adjoining field and follow the grass track close to the hedge, through a couple more gates before reaching the bridle path.

Turn left then left again when you reach the road. Where the road bears right go through the gate into the field on the left and across, keeping close to the hedge on the right. Continue through another gate and finally out through one last gate into the lane. Keep straight ahead down the hill turning right at the bottom back to the pub.

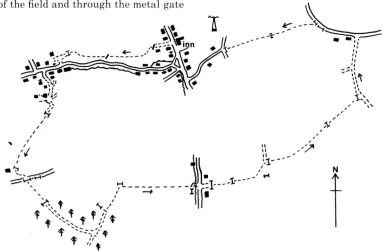